LOVED.

"To love yourself is your job.
It's what you're here for.
And when you do all things are possible."

–

Shiv

To those we love.
You know who you are.

LOVED.

by

VIVIENNE LADOMMATOU
SHAUN YOUNG

How to coach yourself to well-being through self-love

The authors bear no responsibility for any consequences resulting from the use of theinformation contained in this book. All information is used at your own risk.

First paperback edition April 2021

Edited by Effie Charalambous
Layout and cover design by Despina Kannaourou

Published by Hall & Grace Productions Ltd.

hallandgrace.com

HALL & GRACE

Paperback: 978-1-8384788-0-3
Ebook: 978-1-8384788-1-0

ACKNOWLEDGEMENTS

We have many people to thank including all the coaches, psychologists, philosophers and spiritual teachers who have come before us and who have informed, inspired and entertained us on our own journey of self-learning and development. We also want to give special thanks to our families and friends for being there for us, for generously reading manuscripts, sharing thoughts and making suggestions and for just putting up with us.

Above all we want to thank two people without whom this book simply wouldn't be the same. Our designer, Despina Kannaourou, for the look and feel of the whole book including the cover and from whom we learned so much about layout and patience. And our dear friend and editor, Effie Charalambous, who has been so generous with her time and so dedicated to getting it right. We learned so much about why punctuation really matters and we are eternally grateful.

We want you all to know that you are Loved.

Dear Reader,

This book is about you. But first we wanted to share a few things about us and about why we wrote it.

For us, love is not some fluffy, mushy sentiment. It is the vibrational glue that will help us build this new flying machine and manifest our destiny not only as individuals but, as humanity.

There is more than a little poetry to the fact that this book has been so loved and so full of love from the start. To begin with, there is the love and respect we have for each other as co-authors, as colleagues, as friends and as fellow humans. Each of us being and doing the best that we can in our own way, making the best that we can of an imperfect world.

It's also a labor of love. We'd love it if our work turns out to be of interest and value to enough people to make it a best seller. But the key motivator has always been to share with others what we know about the power of self-love and self-coaching after twenty-five years of professional coaching and human psychology.

We've conducted thousands of hours of coaching with thousands of people all over the world and what we have learned is that self-love trumps self-esteem every time. To love yourself and as a result to consciously become the best possible version of you is the single most impactful thing you can do to change your life. And the world. We've been told a pack of lies about how life works. Life doesn't just happen, we make it happen and the most radical thing a person can do to change the world, is to change themselves and to change their mind about how things are.

The intention that created this book is not to advise or tell you what to do, but to provide you with what you need to work it out for yourself. How to be the best you on every level… heart, mind, body and soul. Once we understand that relationship and interaction between these four aspects of being human, we can, with practice, develop insight and mastery over our experience and our lives.

You may or may not have dabbled in self-development before and it may or may not have worked. In any case, what's different about our book is that the focus is on self-love as opposed to self-esteem. And it's an important distinction because self-love is a much more natural and enduring source of personal power and sovereignty.

Loved. provides you with the same framework and coaching questions that we use with our clients to enable you to reflect on what it would take for you as an individual to be well and do well. To identify the gap between where you are now and where you want to be in terms of your physical, cognitive, emotional and spiritual well-being and critically, to do something about it.

All good things,
Vivienne and Shaun

Chapter 1

INTENTION

"The privilege of a lifetime
is to become who you truly are."

–

Carl Jung

Love changes everything. Whatever we look at through the eyes of love transcends all the usual measures of value and is elevated, as if by magic, into something of priceless beauty… a person… a work of art… a purpose fulfilled… a dream realised… a skill mastered. Love is not a feeling or an emotion, it's a force of nature that is more powerful and more capable than any other, of changing the world. We humans express and experience this mysterious energy we call love in many different ways, from the all-encompassing, unconditional love that we feel for our children and that the Greeks call *agape;* to the intoxicating enchantment of *erotas,* of literally falling into a state of blissful abandonment because of the rush of adoration we feel for another person. But we want to focus on an often-ignored way of experiencing and expressing love that is more precious and with more potential to transform than any other. We are talking about the love of self that can and should be the first and most important love of your life.

As we continue to witness the decline of the natural world on which we all depend and as humanity faces unprecedented emergencies, you may feel that self-development is a self-indulgent luxury we can ill afford in times like these. We think the exact opposite is true and believe that now is the best time ever to focus on you. As coaches, we know that people who are conscious of themselves, their thought processes and their impact on others; people who are content, confident in their own abilities, who remain calm and clear headed under pressure, are much more able to live and work together harmoniously. They are also far more likely to find radical and creative solutions to the daunting problems confronting humanity.

If what we want to see is a happier and healthier world for us and for our children and for generations to come, we can be that change by making a conscious choice and commitment to improving the state of our own well-being and as a result, improve the quality of life on Earth. As we have said, our intention is not to tell you what to do but to give you the tools to work it out for yourself.

Loved. offers guidance on how to be well and live a better life and provides a clear pathway of reality creation and self-coaching towards a life that feels… loved.

BEING WELL

"Wellness is the complete integration of body, mind and spirit – the realisation that everything we do, think, feel and believe has an effect on your state of well-being."

–

Greg Anderson

For too long we have delegated responsibility for our personal well-being to others. Looking for answers outside of ourselves, from doctors, dieticians, bloggers, magazine editors and all manner of alternative practitioners, to tell us what's wrong with us and what we should do about it. But it's what *you* think, how *you* feel and what *you* do, that matters. Ultimately, it's *you* who is responsible for knowing what is good or bad for *you* and acting on it.

We're not advising anyone to avoid or delay seeking medical attention or the expertise and advice of physicians and other health professionals. We do believe though, that if we pay more attention to our own body and listen to that quiet, inner voice – the one suggesting you put down the cigarette/doughnut/wine glass, take the stairs, pick up the phone and call your mother, leave the job that makes you miserable, tell the truth – we will need to seek their advice less often. And we'll have more time and energy for the things we care about.

In our current state, we are not only remote and disconnected from our own body – so engrossed are we in the external and virtual worlds – we are also disconnected from our own hearts and minds, with most of us blissfully unaware of what we think about and what's going on in our head when we're not looking.

We would go so far as to say we have literally 'lost our mind' on an individual and collective basis. If you stop for a minute to consider this assertion, you can see evidence of our collective madness wherever you look and if you do take the time to listen objectively to what goes on in your head, you will likely find at least partial madness and chaos there too!

Meanwhile, those of us who feel our minds are in impeccable shape are often disconnected from our feelings. We may well be logical and rational, but we see our body as nothing more than a trolley for our head and we're in our heads so much that over the years, we've lost contact with our hearts. We feel more like an observer than a participant in life. Perhaps most of all, we feel separate and alienated from the spiritual aspect of life and wonder what it even means. We are distracted by the everyday grind of life on Earth and the relentless pressure of covering the cost of living. We are bogged down with meeting the needs of all the others who depend on us and have expectations of us. And managing our social media.

Is that what we really care about? If we weren't so distracted. If we were being our best selves. If we had conscious and compassionate parents, teachers, and leaders. If we felt *loved,* what would life be like? What would *we* be like?

We often spend more time worrying about what other people think, than about what we ourselves think. It's little wonder we rarely take the time to stop and consider if this is the life we really want, let alone to do anything about it.

"The relationship with yourself sets the tone
for every other relationship you have."

–

Jane Travis

Loved. is a blueprint for taking control of every aspect of you and as a result, every area of your life. We often tell our clients "you have the answers" and "all you need to do to find them, is ask the *right* questions". The *right* questions are questions that enable you to see your current point of view, or perspective, on anything that concerns you; from how satisfied you are with the contents of your wardrobe, to why your last relationship ended, why you didn't get that promotion, what you are and are not willing to do for a relative in need, or why you feel so empty and unfulfilled.

Once you become aware of something you are not fully satisfied with, you have two major choices in life: You can choose to *change your mind*, or you can choose to *change your actions*.

When changing your mind, you can choose to hold on to an opinion or perspective that feels right, serves you and/or others and is likely to lead to the desired outcome; or you can choose to change it and see things differently, for a different outcome. Because the old adage is true; when you change the way you look at things, the things you look at change. And from that perspective, everything really is possible.

The world of sport is full of evidence of the power of belief and the truth behind 'where the mind goes the body follows'. As any golfer knows, what goes on in your head is at least as important as what your body does. A champion golfer visualises the ball in the hole or on the green so vividly, that their whole body lines up with the club to deliver that outcome; a high jumper spends several minutes swaying back and forth as they retreat into their 'mind's eye' to 'see' themselves hitting the mattress on the other side of the bar so clearly, that their body believes it can be done and then goes ahead and does it. Once a seemingly impossible barrier is broken by one person, it suddenly becomes much easier for others to follow. Roger Bannister became famous for smashing the four-minute mile in 1954 and it's not by chance that once the psychological obstacle had been lifted, 37 other athletes beat the same record within the next two years.

You will have had similar experiences at times and in some areas of your life, with or without knowing it. You will have created your reality through the power of belief, for better or for worse and you will have experienced the sense of pure 'being-ness' that comes when we are absolutely present in the here and now. That magical place where everything is in *flow* and all things are possible.

We all know what it feels like to be *connected* in the *zone* or in 'flow'. For example, you wake up feeling refreshed just before the alarm and 'get out of the right side of the bed', you crack an egg for breakfast and it has a double yolk, you make all the green lights on the way to work, circumstances seem to conspire to support you and everything seems to be *happening for you;* you either make no mistakes or you benefit when you do and you choose options that serve you. You are your own ally and your own best friend.

At the same time, we all know on some level that there are at least some areas of our life where things are not working, where we do things that we don't want to do and don't do things that we do want to do. We know what it feels like to be 'disconnected' and out of 'flow'. For example, you wake up with a jolt before you're really ready and get out of the 'wrong side of the bed', you crack an egg for breakfast and break the yolk, every traffic light in the city seems to be on red, circumstances seem to conspire to hinder and obstruct you and everything seems to be happening to you. You feel victimised, make silly mistakes and reach for too many biscuits or too many glasses of wine. You are your own worst enemy.

It's often at this point that people seek out somebody to talk to – a friend, a family member, or maybe a coach. We're always happy to hear from a new client, but wouldn't it be great if you didn't need us? In many ways that's the ultimate intention of this book, to outline what we do as coaches in a clear and simple process, so that you can do it for yourself.

We've watched thousands of people create the reality that they want and we've observed many more thousands consistently create what they don't want! Wherever you are, whatever you do, whether or not you are conscious of it and whether or not you want the result that you get, you are in your own process of reality creation.

REALITY CREATION

"At the moment of commitment,
the entire universe conspires to assist you."

–

Goethe

For us, this quote says it all. Reality creation is actually a co-creation that involves the physical and metaphysical realms. And it is also a process that involves what you think, what you feel and crucially, what you do.

Like the power of prayer or fibre optics, it's not necessary to understand why it works in order for it to work. And although belief is, as you will discover, an important part of reality creation, for now, all we ask is that you suspend any disbelief for long enough to give it a chance. You have nothing to lose and literally, everything to gain!

We are all co-creating our reality all the time, we're just not aware of it. If we want to be in control and create reality *consciously*, in addition to opening up to it as a possibility, we also need to change the way we look at failure.

We are often puzzled by the fact that we can be so successful in one or two areas of our life and such a 'failure' in others. But there's no such thing as failure, only feedback on how close the results are to the goal or desired outcome. Whether or not this feedback contributes to our ultimate success depends on how resilient we are on our ability to bounce back. When we are resilient and we don't hit the target, we reflect on the insights gained and adjust our actions accordingly, until we do. This is how intelligence (also athletes and concert pianists) evolves, so how come we have little if any respect for failure?

To succeed, you have to be willing to fail or as Joe Vitale of *Law of Attraction* fame puts it, 'you have to be willing to suck'. In other words, you have to have the courage and compassion to risk doing your thing badly, in order for you to be in with a chance of doing your thing really well.

Resilience is an important part of reality creation and how resilient we are depends to a large extent on the state of our well-being and how well we feel on every level. We can all recognise that whenever we are struggling on a physical, mental, emotional, or spiritual level, we are less resilient, less resourceful, less creative and often, less courageous and compassionate to self and others. We are also a lot less likely to take action and achieve our goals.

Logically, we can see that the solutions to at least some of our own problems are simple and yet we don't deal with it. We get the insight but are missing the other half of the success equation, which is the action. Building resilience through self-coaching and self-care is the answer and this book shows you how.

First, we want to show you how you can consciously co-create your reality through a step-by-step process that has a track record of success and is based on the findings of someone much smarter than we are.

"Logic will get you from A to B,
imagination will take you everywhere."

–

Albert Einstein

Everything that ever was, is, or ever will be, began with a thought. Einstein, unarguably one of our greatest scientists, understood that. He also knew that we live in a world of finite energy and infinite potential and that the only way into the field of infinite potential, is through the imagination, *"Imagination is everything..."*, he said, *"...it is the preview of life's coming attractions"*.

He saw no chasm between what science knows and the mystery of creation. He saw everything as part of the whole and seemed quite comfortable holding the tension between two seemingly opposing ideas, like science and spirituality. And so are we. There is no chasm and we love the way the authors of Spontaneous Evolution, Bruce Lipton and Steve Bhaerman, put it, *"Science has climbed the mountain of knowledge and found Buddha sitting at the top"*.

We are constantly imagining things that turn up in our lives, even if we aren't aware of it and it's not always what we want. This is because of the human condition of negative thinking. We are all predisposed to things like worrying unnecessarily about things that haven't happened or refusing to believe something until we can see it, often in order to hedge our bets and protect ourselves from disappointment... we even offer each other advice to *hope for the best and prepare for the worst!* It's in this way we create self-fulfilling prophecies. We imagine or have a thought about something... let's say we begin to suspect that our new love is not being entirely honest with us. Something they say or do triggers something that makes us doubt their interest in us, or it might be because their name is Sam and we once dated someone called Sam who turned out to be a cheat. In any case, the seed of doubt has been planted and it begins to grow into a small shoot of mistrust. We start to question what they say as we wonder if they are being truthful. We focus our attention on trying to catch them out and ask rather too many questions about their movements when we are not together and become distracted by our doubts and less engaged when we are. Before we know it, the shoot of mistrust grows into a big thorny bush and our love grows tired of the suspicion and turns to another for support. Our worst fears are confirmed when they tell us it's over and we tell ourselves and all our friends to never even think about dating another Sam! We constantly and inadvertently create undesired outcomes in our lives because we are unconscious of the fact that every thought, feeling and action, is an act of co-creation between us and all the other creative forces that exist in this dimension.

To consciously co-create reality is to realise – *to make real* – an intention or idea through a very distinct process involving the acknowledgment of your connection to everything, the power of your imagination, your ability to believe it before you see it and the actions you take to confirm this. In other words, to receive is not a passive act, it's an outcome that requires our attention and involves acceptance of our role as co-creator and an alignment of what we *think*, what we *feel* and crucially, what we *do*.

A word about *connection* as the first and most fundamental step in the process of consciously co-creating reality. It's more of a switch than a step and it's a switch that is 'always on'. We are always connected to the 'magic' of reality creation because we *are* the magic! Whenever we attempt to connect with something that we perceive as being outside of ourselves, we are denying our natural state as an integral part of it. We are literally achieving the opposite of the desired effect.

This connection goes hand in hand with a heightened sense of self that could be described as authenticity and which is actually an act of acceptance of self as both the experience and expression of Source (the Universe, God, All That Is, Nature etc.). You cannot connect to something of which you are already a part. To connect with your Source (however or whatever you perceive it to be), all you have to do is to simply acknowledge and be consciously aware of already being a part of it.

SELF-COACHING

"When you change the way you look at things,
the things you look at change."

–

Max Planck

A good coach partners with you to create the reality that you want by exploring your inner dialogue. They will often advise you to observe your thoughts and make notes. They'll ask if you like what you hear yourself say? How does it make you feel? How does it impact your behaviour? Do you want to listen to it for the rest of your life or would you like to change it? You can ask these questions of yourself and in this book, we will show you how.

Coaching is not what you think it is; it's not about fixing yourself or anyone else. Coaching is an attitude that we can adopt with ourselves and with others to promote growth and realise potential. It's also a process of exploration and of looking at challenges and opportunities from different angles, to deepen understanding, gain clarity, make choices and plan actions. In short, a coach creates the space and framework for you to get to know yourself better, decide what you want and plan how to achieve it.

This book is designed to do the same. To provide you with the space, framework and questions to hear yourself think, to understand your feelings and the relationship between your thoughts, feelings and behaviour and to clarify how this relates to your experience and results.

If the idea of hearing yourself think is new to you, it's important to understand that, whether or not you are conscious of it, there are a number of things going on in your head that you may not be aware of and self-coaching is one way of becoming more consciously aware and therefore, in control of them.

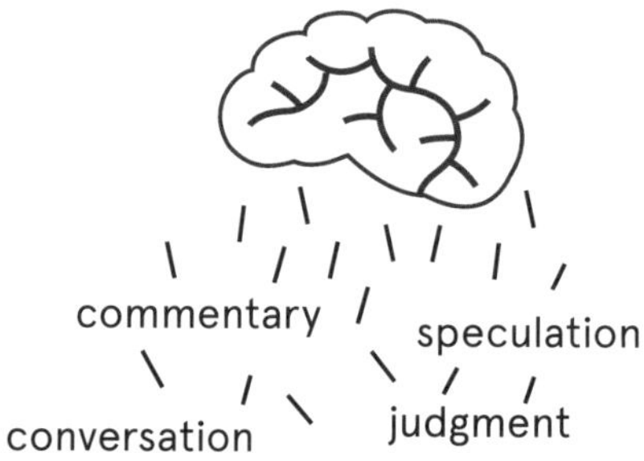

We all talk to ourselves, it's the first sign of sanity! We're all talking about different things, but we all have the same processes. This inner dialogue has various aspects, one of which is a running narrative called *commentary*. Just as a soccer match has a commentator and a documentary has a narrator, we commentate or narrate our own life. Your commentary can either feel like it is coming directly from you (as if you are saying the words in your mind), or it can feel like you're listening passively – like listening to the radio. Either way, becoming consciously aware of it gives you a peek into your habitual thinking and belief systems. It is this insight that gives you the opportunity to *change your mind*, which potentially changes everything.

It is the quality of our commentary on life that, to a large degree, determines how we experience life. Some of us can be quite harsh with our commentary, criticising ourselves, other people, different opinions and the whole world! All of which has a negative impact on how we think, feel and behave. Some of us are real comedians, laughing at things even when we shouldn't be – and this helps us to stay light and keep smiling. While we all tend to shift through various styles of commentary, we also have a 'default' setting where we spend most of our time.

Another aspect of our inner dialogue is *speculation*. As naturally curious human beings, it is inevitable that we wonder about things, ask questions and weigh up possibilities. *What do people think of me? Will I look stupid? What's my role in life? What if it doesn't work? How should I handle this situation? What if I don't do as she asks? What is he thinking? What's the meaning of life?*

It is also inevitable that on the back of this speculation we form *judgments* (answers, opinions) that can be positive, negative, or neutral. It is the quality of these conversations, of this inner dialogue, that dictates how you experience and express life, as well as what we can achieve and the impact that we have. *People don't understand me. They think I look stupid. I'm in the wrong role. I can do something different. All I need to do is be myself. If I explain my side of the story, she will see my point. I will ask what he's thinking and find out, he might have a good idea. The meaning of life is to love and be loved.*

So, we have *conversations* with ourselves all the time in our own heads. And we also have them with other people. Before we speak to somebody, we prepare in our head what we want to say and we respond as if we are the other person, even somebody we've never met. This results in an imaginary conversation during which we make various assumptions about what they think or feel and about their intentions.

We repeat conversations over and over in our heads, embellishing them with our imagination. We often make imaginary conversations so real in our own minds, that we then live them out in reality by unconsciously allowing them to impact how we relate and respond to others.

Becoming aware of this inner dialogue is what gives us the opportunity to explore the relationship between our thoughts, feelings and behaviour and underscores the fact that we are the creators of our reality… not just our subjective reality but at least to some extent, our objective reality too. For example, if you *think* that something is impossible, you then *feel* that it's impossible and you will then *behave* as if it's not possible. The results you then get, reinforce your original belief by providing you with the evidence to support it. This is how expectation impacts reality and how, when used consciously, the concept of a 'self-fulfilling prophecy' can play out in our lives to produce the desired outcome. David Beckham was reportedly told by his father from the age of two that he was going to play centre forward for Manchester United.

"Whether you think you can,
or you think you can't, you're right."

–

Henry Ford

We are creating our experience of life from moment to moment on very subtle levels. One of the many benefits of being aware of and taking control of your inner dialogue is that you recognise those subtleties and can work with them to achieve what you want in life.

So, the big questions we'd like to help you to answer are…

What reality are you creating for yourself?
What reality are you creating for others?
What reality would you like to create?

In the next chapter we introduce you to our *love-orientated self-coaching process* that you can use when you're working on your well-being.

The third chapter 'Get Well, Be Well' is all about working on your physical, cognitive, emotional, and spiritual intelligence. You will be working on all four, but you decide in what order. You may choose the topic that you're most interested in or that you feel you most need to work on first. There is a self-assessment at the end of each intelligence to help you identify your strengths and areas for development and this is supported by techniques that we have been using for years, with great success, with ourselves and our clients.

REALISATION PRACTICES: Designed to raise your awareness about all aspects of your well-being.

MIRROR MOMENTS: Big coaching questions that help you to reflect in the moment and identify key learning and insights.

In the fourth and final chapter, we explore what it means to 'Do Well', and how love and being *loved*, is not some fluffy, mushy sentiment, but the vibrational glue that will help us build this new flying machine and manifest our destiny not only as individuals, but as humanity.

Now's the time to take a few moments to consider what you want to take away from this process. Without limiting your aspirations to what you think is possible, or what you believe you can achieve, or feel you deserve, what would you *really* like to get out of this? What would it mean for you to be the best version of you? What would be different? Go beyond your expectations and think about the greatest potential: What do you want to have, how do you want to be at the end of this book?

Chapter 2

SELF LOVE

"Anytime we can listen to true self
and give the care it requires,
we do it not only for ourselves,
but for the many others whose lives we touch."

-

Parker Palmer

First we need to make the distinction between self-love and self-esteem. The path of self-development has been firmly focused on self-esteem, but this often has little to do with self-love and everything to do with being in competition, not only with others, but with ourselves. In other words, self-esteem is a value judgment.

Self-love is an overall acceptance of who you are, including your flaws. It's what motivates you to cherish and take care of yourself, to focus on what makes you feel happy and *loved.*

Self-esteem is an evaluation of self-worth that is often based on comparison to others and the idea that in order to have high self-esteem, we have to feel that we are somehow better than others. Whether we are aware of it or not, most of us habitually compare ourselves to others. We even play games to big ourselves up or make others feel small because we need to make ourselves feel better than others in order to feel better about ourselves.

So distorted is our sense of what it means to be ourselves, that we have forgotten what it means to love ourselves. Social media and our retreat in to a selfie-obsessed culture, rigged with filters and Photoshop, fake tans and facial fillers, all feeds our fixation with feeling good because of how well we compare to others. All too often, this means we need to look like a completely different person, living a completely different life. We post a picture that makes us look prettier, more handsome, thinner, fitter, more successful and it gives us a hit of the pleasure hormone, dopamine. We check for 'likes' every ten minutes and when we get them we get more dopamine… and when we don't we often feel the need to resort to more extreme measures, like cutting up our bodies to gain approval, or racking up more debt in order to look happy on holiday for *'the gram',* when in fact, our relationship is falling apart.

Most of us intuitively know that love is a better strategy for becoming the best version of ourselves, but we still rely on criticism and fear of criticism from others in order to improve. We believe we need it to motivate us. We fear that if we feel good enough as we are, we won't strive to get better. But research shows the opposite is true. Cortisol is the stress hormone and every time we're under pressure and feel criticised we release cortisol and that increases our stress levels. This is a part of a chemical reaction we call 'fight or flight' that we once needed to survive the threat of lions and tigers and poisonous snakes. Criticism is a *perceived* threat. Criticism is not going to do the same damage as a tiger, but the body doesn't know that and the physical reaction is basically the same. We are usually unaware that this is happening and we think we're coping, but our body is taking the strain. Stress is a modern disease that has vast implications for our health and well-being. Some doctors maintain that stress is the starting point of all illness, physical and mental.

Some people can harness stress and use it to become champion athletes or virtuoso violinists. But it's not easy to manage high levels of stress consistently over long periods of time without the risk of burnout. For most of us, stress is debilitating. More stress and more cortisol lead to more mistakes, less trust in our own judgment and more fear and anxiety. When the body is flooded with too much cortisol and increased feelings of anxiety, its coping mechanism is to shut down or withdraw into depression. So, we know for a fact that the pressure we exert on ourselves through habitual self-criticism does not motivate us. In fact it leads to higher levels of cortisol, higher levels of anxiety and lower levels of motivation.

"Self love offers the benefits of self esteem without the pitfalls!"

-

Kristin Neff

Self-love is the natural, more stable alternative to the precarious treadmill of self-esteem. It has nothing to do with the constant comparison to others or striving to be better all the time and has everything to do with accepting, nurturing and celebrating what we already are, on every level. We're warm-blooded creatures and when we feel loved and accepted, we respond with the release of the feel-good hormones' oxytocin and opiates. We feel happier, more motivated, more connected and more capable of serving ourselves and others. This leads to better lifestyle choices, healthier relationships and a lot less stress, anxiety and depression.

If you think it's selfish to love yourself, think again. Research shows that the more love and compassion we have for self, the more love and compassion we have for others. In her book *Daring Greatly,* social scientist Brene Brown talks about how to live 'wholeheartedly' by giving up the need to be perfect and instead embracing our imperfections.

According to Brené, wholehearted living is about engaging in our lives from a place of self-acceptance and the belief that we are worthy of love. It's about owning our story and accepting that we are imperfect and vulnerable. To feel worthy of love, she says, takes courage, compassion, and connection.

Courage is about being vulnerable and being your true self. Compassion is about accepting yourself and others as equals. Connection with others is the natural by-product of these. We feel strong, resilient and ready for anything when we feel Loved.

"Do you want to meet the love of your life?
Look in the mirror."

-

Byron Katie

We need to find love not from others but from ourselves. Self-love is about valuing ourselves and our lives *no matter what.* It's about spending quality time with oneself, allowing time to find inner harmony and peace. It's about experiencing fulfilment and meaning in your life; not when you've won the lottery, found the right partner, or been offered the perfect job, but right now, in this and every moment.

This type of love resides inside of us all. It feels familiar and instinctive because on a deeper level we all know how to give and receive unconditional love. We feel it when we empathise with someone, when we feel what they feel, when we truly see them without judgment and when, regardless of what a person has done, we still love them with all our being. That is what we need and deserve to feel from ourselves too.

Now let's take a look at what happens when we apply self-love to everyday life by listening to ourselves with love, asking loving questions and giving advice from a place of unconditional love. We all know what it feels like to give others good advice but when it comes to advising ourselves, it's not as simple. Why is it so difficult to be loving and caring when it's all about us?

"You can't solve a problem
with the same mindset that created it."

-

Albert Einstein

We believe that people do have the resources and love within them to meet their own needs – it's just a matter of accessing them. Here's how to step out of yourself and your mindset through a process of self-coaching that will help you find the answers you seek and also boost your self-love.

Imagine your 10-year-old child or if you're not a parent, imagine a child that you love and care about and for whom you are responsible at this time. Imagine they come home from school and ask you to do their maths homework for them. What's the first thought that enters your head? What's the first thing you say? Do you say, 'yes give it here I'm really good at maths and I can do that for you in 10 minutes, you go and get a juice and watch some TV'? If you did, it would make most 10-year olds really happy and establish you as their new best friend, but it's probably not what you would say, is it? You are more likely to be curious and to ask a few questions about why they can't do their own homework, right? You want to know what stops them, what's missing? And the reason you want to know is because you care about them and their development and you don't want them to become dependent on you. It's love in action and all you need to do is to bring that kind of unconditional love and curiosity to your self-coaching in order to know what to ask, what to say and ultimately, to know… *what would love do?*

BE YOUR OWN COACH

"If you wish your life were different...
do your life differently."
-
Terence Houlihan

What Would Love Do? is a love-based coaching model. You can use this 4-step process, through the lens of love, to find your own answers to life's challenges and opportunities.

For this technique to be really effective, you need to step outside of yourself so that the challenges you're having are not yours. The idea is to think and act as if you're giving advice to someone you love unconditionally and hold in high regard. The kind of love we feel towards a child or a parent. This may take some practice but it does get easier and the takeout from looking at things differently, without judgment and self-criticism, is well worth it.

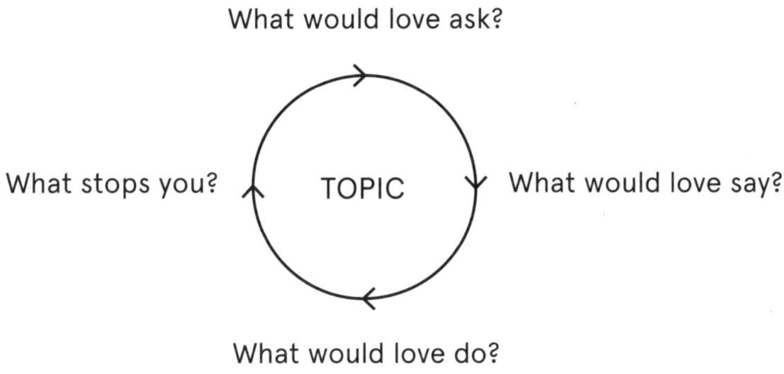

WHAT WOULD LOVE DO?

A love orientated exploratory dialogue…

To start self-coaching, identify a topic you would like to work with. It can be anything that you would like to change in your life, or it could be a New Year resolution that seems to come up every year. Write a short opening statement that best describes it. For example, I want more balance in my life, I seem to spend less time on the things that I love and too much time working.

Now focus on your chosen topic in *a love orientated exploratory dialogue* by imagining you are talking to a loved one who has come to you for advice and support. Go through each step, asking and answering questions in your inner dialogue, until you feel you have completed your self-coaching and are satisfied with the outcome. Depending on the topic, this might take several cycles with answers like 'I don't know' or "I'm not sure" that present themselves as apparent obstacles. But they're not obstacles, they are simply what's true for you, at this moment, in response to that question.

It's important to trust the process and keep going through the cycle because it's an exploration and it's okay if you don't have the answers straight away. Just give yourself enough time and space to observe your inner dialogue, with all it's judgments, limiting beliefs and frustrations. Work with whatever comes up for you including any doubts, perceived lack of progress, or questions and answers you may not find satisfying.

If, for example, your response to "What's stopping you?" in Step 4 is "I don't know", then you go back to Step 1 and simply ask them (yourself) whatever you would naturally ask a loved one if they had said "I don't know".

STEP 1: What would love ask?

Imagine it's a loved one and not yourself that you're talking to and that it's *their* topic. If the aim of this step is to know what the 'other person' wants, what question/s do you want to ask in order to understand? And how would you answer each of those question/s?

E.g. Topic 'I feel inadequate and incapable of home-schooling my son.'
Q: What is it that makes you feel inadequate?
A: Not being able to get him to do anything without bribery.

STEP 2: What would love say?

Imagine it's a loved one and not yourself that you're talking to and it's *their* answer/s, what would you say in response and how would you say it?

E.g. You do know you're not alone and there's whole articles about this in every newspaper and magazine and dozens of YouTube videos.

STEP 3: What would love do?

Imagine it's a loved one and not yourself that you're talking to and it's *their* topic you are offering advice on, what would you advise them to do?

E.g. Read about the experiences of other parents and watch videos that they have made about how they deal with it. That way you will feel less alone and get the benefit of their experience and advice.

STEP 4: What stops you?

Based on this inner dialogue, what stops you from taking your own advice and acting from a place of self-love? If nothing is stopping you, then all you need to do is take action. *If something is stopping you, go back to Step 1 and repeat the cycle – but focus on your answer to this question – until you know what to do, how and when to do it and there's nothing else stopping you.*

E.g. If the answer to this question is 'lack of time, I'm too busy making a hash of my son's education'. Examples of the questions you might ask are, 'What stops you from making the time?' and 'How can you find the time'?

When using this process of self-coaching through inner dialogue, you may find the answers you're looking for first-time. Or you may need to repeat the process several times before you get there. If you find yourself coming up with the same response to more than one question, just see it as part of the process. Like all good coaching, it's about exploration and there are no wrong answers.

What's important is to get into the habit of looking at your life and all its challenges and opportunities, through the lens of love. The more you do this, the more accomplished you will become at practicing self-love and as a result, the more you will feel that you're living a life that's Loved.

Here are some examples of how a self-coaching conversation might look and feel. Each example relates to one of the four 'realms' or 'aspects' of being human – physical, cognitive, emotional and spiritual – we'll explain more about these in the next chapter.

GAINING WEIGHT

Topic: I've gained weight and I need to do something about it, but I don't feel motivated.

STEP 1: What would love ask?
Q: Why is your weight a problem for you? What do you want to happen?
A: It makes me feel fat and ugly and I want to feel attractive.
STEP 2: What would love say?
It's a natural part of getting older, don't worry about it and instead eat healthy, cut down on the alcohol and exercise more. I can help you!
STEP 3: What would love do?
Cut down on alcohol, crisps and cakes and make the time to exercise at least three times a week on a regular basis.
STEP 4: What's stopping you?
Lack of time and motivation.
>
STEP 1: What would love ask?
Q: What would help you to make the time and feel more motivated?
A: Watch less television and find a way to combine exercise with spending time with family and friends.
STEP 2: What would love say?
Brilliant, sounds like a good idea.
STEP 3: What would love do?
Make a plan that involves exercise before television and that invites and enables friends and family to join in.
STEP 4: What's stopping you?
Nothing, I even have a plan!

BEATING MYSELF UP

Topic: I am my worst critic and I would like to stop telling myself off.

STEP 1: What would love ask?

Q: Why do you criticise yourself so much?

A: Because I know I can be better.

STEP 2: What would love say?

None of us is perfect and we can all improve – that's what we are here for.

STEP 3: What would love do?

Listen to your inner dialogue. When you hear self-criticism, choose to stop and instead talk to yourself like a good friend.

STEP 4: What's stopping you?

I'll forget in the heat of the moment.

>

STEP 1: What would love ask?

Q: What happens when you're in the heat of the moment?

A: I get frustrated and start fixating on the mistakes I think I made or what I could have done better.

STEP 2: What would love say?

It's okay to make mistakes, that's how we learn.

STEP 3: What would love do?

The next time you get frustrated and start fixating on what you did 'wrong'. Make a conscious effort to take control of your thoughts, be compassionate and tell yourself that it's okay and that everybody makes mistakes. Talk to yourself as a good friend and ask what you learned from the experience?

STEP 4: What's stopping you?

Nothing, I'm up for the challenge!

TOXIC RELATIONSHIP
Topic: I want my husband to change his ways.

STEP 1: What would love ask?
Q: What frustrates you?
A: He doesn't help me with the housework.
STEP 2: What would love say?
You need to tell him how you feel, listen to his point of view and talk about a solution.
STEP 3: What would love do?
Be true to yourself and tell him how you feel
STEP 4: What's stopping you?
I'm afraid he won't listen and get angry
>
STEP 1: What would love ask?
Q: What is the worst that can happen?
A: He will hit me again.
STEP 2: What would love say?
That must be so difficult, what can I do to help?
STEP 3: What would love do?
Advise them to leave.
STEP 4: What's stopping you?
I love him and my children even though it's difficult.
>
STEP 1: What would love ask?
Q: What do you want to happen now?
A: I want to give him a chance to change his ways and try counselling.
STEP 2: What would love say?
I hope you find the courage and strength to speak to him and leave if you have to for the good of you and the whole family.

STEP 3: What would love do?
Have the conversation in a public place to reduce the risk of a flare up and in case it gets out of hand, have somewhere safe to go.
STEP 4: What's stopping you?
Yes, good plan but I always get flustered and forget what I want to say.
>
STEP 1: What would love ask?
Q: What would help you to stay calm and know what to say?
A: Write it down and practice.
STEP 2: What would love say?
That's a brilliant idea, how can I help?
STEP 3: What would love do?
Decide what you want to say, write it down and rehearse it with me or a friend.
STEP 4: What's stopping you?
Nothing except fear, but this time I won't let it stop me.

THE RIGHT PATH
Topic: I feel that I'm on the wrong path, but I'm not sure what the 'right' path is.

STEP 1: What would love ask?
Q: What makes you think you are on the wrong path?
A: I feel unfulfilled and like something is missing in my life.
STEP 2: What would love say?
That must be difficult, you deserve to feel fulfilled and satisfied with your life.
STEP 3: What would love do?
Be mindful of what really matters to you and take steps towards it.
STEP 4: What's stopping you?
A mortgage.
>

STEP 1: What would love ask?
Q: How can you pay your mortgage and live a life that is meaningful to you?
A: Downsize, reduce my work hours and give myself space to find out what really matters to me.
STEP 2: What would love say?
How exciting, that sounds like a plan and now you can start thinking about different paths that might be right for you.
STEP 3: What would love do?
Look for a cheaper place to live where you would be happy, speak to them at work and start planning.
STEP 4: What's stopping you?
Nothing, I'm going to stop off at the estate agents on the way home.

Be honest in your inner dialogue, notice the quality of the relationship you are having with yourself. Are you your best friend or worst enemy? Think about your answers, feel your answers, write about, or talk to others about your answers, or go straight to turning insight into action and as they say… *just do it!*

We know from our own direct experience of using this technique on thousands of people and on ourselves that you can feel more supported by yourself, more loved, happier, less stressed and less alone. Once we have learned how to truly be there for ourselves, we can then help others to do the same.

This is a technique that you will get to practice throughout this handbook. Give it a go the next time you feel you need a little love.

Chapter 3

GET WELL, BE WELL

"To understand the whole, it is necessary
to understand the parts. To understand the parts,
it is necessary to understand the whole."

-

Ken Wilber

When we see ourselves as a system made up of four, constituent parts, it's immediately apparent that everything about us is interconnected. We also realise that being well as a whole is going to mean giving attention to all four parts, with self-love as both the driver and the outcome.

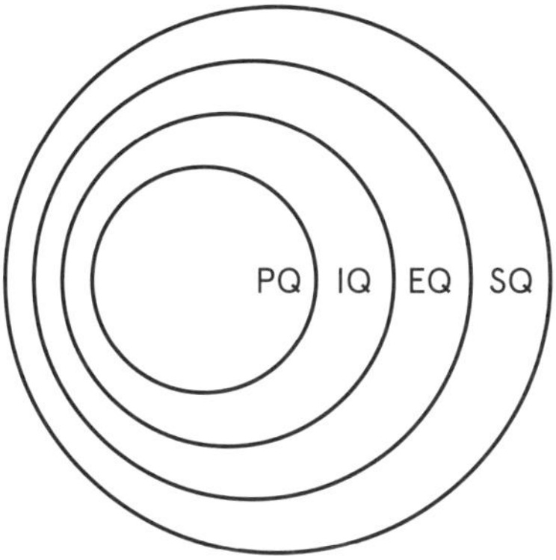

The model illustrates the four parts of being human in a holarchy of human intelligence; physical (PQ), cognitive (IQ), emotional (EQ) and spiritual (SQ). A holarchy is distinct from a hierarchy in that the whole transcends and includes each of its parts. This holarchy is basically a representation of how the physical, cognitive, emotional and spiritual aspects of being human integrate as a whole. In relation to personal development, our physical health is foundational to our cognitive and emotional health, which combine to enable our spiritual growth and well-being.

Having *integral intelligence* means being consciously aware of all aspects of self and of the interconnectedness of all things, including the four realms of being human. This involves being more intentional about our thoughts, feelings and behaviour and conscious of everything we do, including our daily routines and practices. The purpose of the Realisation Practices, Mirror Moments and everything else in this book, is to give you a framework for becoming conscious and intentional about well-being and about developing integral intelligence, as an expression of self-love.

We can go beyond personal development and apply the integral lens to life in general. For example, the integral way of preparing for an exam or interview, is to focus not only on what you need to know cognitively and be mentally prepared, but to also be conscious of how prepared you are physically and emotionally. Have you had enough sleep and rest? How well are you managing your stress levels? How confident do you feel? There's no obvious link to spiritual intelligence in this example, but your self-love and the extent to which you trust the Universe to 'have your back' when you're under pressure, is a measure of your spiritual well-being. It's recognising and understanding that it is all aspects of you, all four realms, that contribute to your successes and to your failures.

Using cognitive and emotional awareness to choose how you want to increase your physical well-being through exercise, is another example of how to apply integral thinking in everyday life. It takes into account not just the desired outcome (getting rid of the spare around your midriff, not getting puffed halfway up the stairs, being able to touch your toes again) but also the positive impact it will have on your mental agility, emotional well-being and overall quality of life, if you take up an exercise or activity that is right for you.

Conscious eating is evidence of an integral lifestyle and is about understanding food as more than just fuel or entertainment for your body and good nutrition as an act of self-love. It's not just what you eat but where, when, how and why you eat, that impacts how you experience food, as well as how food impacts you on a physical, emotional, cognitive and spiritual level. Meanwhile, observing your everyday life through an integral lens and asking the right questions of yourself, can offer insight into what's behind the less tangible more spiritual challenges in life, like the sense of emptiness and lack of meaning or purpose that we all sometimes feel.

Whatever you want to develop in your life, it's more satisfying, more sustainable and believe it or not, easier to develop it from an integral or holistic perspective. The reason it's easier is because the nature of the universe and the way that nature works is integral and holistic. It's also abundant and limitless. All we need to do to access this abundance is to believe this is true before we see the evidence. This is because *where the mind goes the body follows.* It's how Tiger Woods gets a hole in one, how Sabrina Williams wins Grand Slams and how sociopaths and narcissists get to the top.

PHYSICAL

"Most people have no idea how good
their body is designed to feel."

-

Kevin Trudeau

The way we define physical intelligence, or PQ, is through four main elements: *Body Awareness, Nourishment, Fitness* and *Rest.*

BODY AWARENESS – how we relate to our body, body language, posture
NOURISHMENT – being a conscious consumer
FITNESS – stamina, strength, flexibility and breath
REST – the importance of taking time out and getting quality sleep

Physical intelligence is about more than maintaining physical health and well-being by making it a habit to eat well, rest well and take regular exercise. Having said that, the importance of physical health and well-being cannot be overestimated and ill health impacts absolutely every other area of our life, from how we feel in ourselves, to what we can achieve and contribute.

Having physical intelligence means you know and respond to your physical needs and understand how your own body language impacts both you and others. The indicators of physical intelligence include a high level of body awareness, attention to good nutrition and a commitment to regular exercise that you enjoy, as well as getting enough rest including good quality sleep.

It also means taking a broader, integral view of physical well-being. Through this lens, movement of the body is not just about fitness; physical activity is also an excellent way to reduce stress and promote well-being. Most people want to exercise, or at least know that it would be very good for them if they did. The number one reason why most people say they don't exercise, is lack of time. The truth is that the biggest factor or obstacle to regular exercise is usually just a lack of commitment… not making the choice to focus on what matters. And what matters more than your physical well-being? The same is true of good eating habits. The information about good nutrition is either well known to us or readily available. But that doesn't mean we act on it. *We choose whether or not we make good nutrition a priority.*

We seem to take the same approach to rest, seeing it as something that would be nice to have but which simply isn't an option! Yet it's common knowledge that rest and sleep really matter and that the quality and quantity of our sleep impacts both how we feel and what we can achieve in the short term, as well as our health, well-being and even our longevity in the long term. Even without fully understanding the nature of sleep, we know that going without sleep makes us feel terrible, while getting a good night's sleep on a regular basis can change everything and make us feel ready for anything.

"The only difference between people who live in the magic of life and those who do not is that those who live in the magic of life have habituated certain ways of being."

-

Marci Shimoff

Physical intelligence is foundational and impacts all the other intelligences or realms of being human, from our ability to think straight, to our emotional strength and our resilience in the face of adversity. As the old adage goes, it's important to look after your body… after all, it's where you live!

How physically intelligent are you? Here are the four elements of physical intelligence in more detail, followed by some self-coaching questions to help you reflect on how satisfied you are with your current level of physical intelligence.

BODY AWARENESS

"Health is a relationship between you
and your body."

-

Terri Guillemets

Body awareness is a term that has a number of different interpretations. For the purposes of this book, body awareness is about how we relate to our body. How aware are you of your own body? Are you the kind of person who treats your body as little more than a trolley for getting your head to meetings? Or do you listen to your body and partner with it to ensure it gets what it needs to be in peak condition?

For us, body awareness means being in touch or in tune with our body and being conscious of how we feel on a physical level, as well as how we make others feel through our physical presence, posture and body language.

It's less obvious and often ignored that body awareness is closely linked to the strategy of 'fake it until you make it' or 'acting as if'.

From Steven Covey in his seminal work, *The 7 Habits*, to rock-star coach, Tony Robbins in *Unlimited Power*, to Deepak Chopra in the *7 Spiritual Laws of Success;* people who are really good at human development agree that *the body believes what the mind tells it*… If you're not already convinced of this, try imagining yourself slicing open a fresh lemon on a chopping board. As you slice it open, smell the fragrance of the zest and then imagine yourself picking up one half and notice what actually happens in your mouth as you imagine biting into it.

Just as important is the fact that, not only does your body believe what your mind tells it, *your mind listens to what your body says* through posture, body language, facial expressions and gestures. It's not difficult to make yourself depressed. It takes a lot of effort but anyone can do it. If you walk around with slouched shoulders, a sad expression and downward gaze for long enough, you literally become it. And you can even screw up your bio-system by choosing to put things in your body that will give you low blood sugar and almost guarantee your depression. Basically, your body language impacts everyone and it especially impacts you!

Posture tends to be the most obvious and enduring aspect of our body language and refers to the position the body assumes during various activities like sitting, standing and walking. A good standing posture is what enables the body to work well with forces of nature like gravity and ground reaction. It also minimizes the wear and tear of joints and soft tissue and reduces the risk of injury. Good posture also feels good. Do a basic assessment of your own posture by standing against a wall in bare feet, with your feet together, pointing straight ahead and with your heels, buttocks, shoulders and head touching the wall. It should look and feel completely natural and your bodyweight should be positioned towards the outside of your heels.

If your posture doesn't look or feel right, it's important to find the right kind of expert to help you adjust it. If, for example, during the above assessment you feel pressure at the front of your feet and in your toes, it may mean that your bodyweight is falling forward and you will have to compensate by pushing down with your toes in order to stay balanced. An expert can help you to understand these less obvious aspects of posture and how the body compensates for one area of dysfunction, by overusing other areas and will advise you on what to do about it.

Irrespective of whether or not you feel the need to consult an expert about your posture, you can start training yourself now to be more consciously aware of your own posture.

REALISATION PRACTICE: *Fly On The Wall*

Ask someone at work or at home to use your phone to film you for 60 seconds doing normal things, like walking into a room, interacting with other people, sitting at a desk and generally going about your daily life. Ask someone you feel comfortable being yourself with and do your best to ignore them and the camera. What you are looking for is a 'fly on the wall' perspective.

You may find it difficult to act naturally when you are being watched. 60 seconds may feel like a long time, but stick with it, because looking back at yourself will provide you with invaluable information about your relationship with your body that you can't get any other way.

We recommend you review the footage twice. The first time is just a preview when you'll focus mainly on whether or not you like what you're wearing, how thin, fat, young or old you think you look and whether or not you like your own face or hair. The second time look beyond the aesthetics and focus only on what your body is saying.

- What messages are you getting from your body language; what do you notice about your posture, facial expressions and mannerisms?
- What impact would you say your body language has on the way you feel on the inside?
- What messages do you think others are getting from your body language?
- How would you like to adapt your body language for a different result?

MIRROR MOMENT: *Body Talk*

When you are in partnership with your body, you relate to it differently. You don't ignore it. From this perspective, in this moment, what is your body telling you? What will you do about it?

NOURISHMENT

"Let thy food be thy medicine
and thy medicine be thy food."
-
Hippocrates

When we talk about food and nutrition in relation to well-being, all too often the conversation is limited to food groups and portion sizes, whether or not this or that makes you thin or fat and what is and is not good or bad for you. We'd like to focus on good nutrition from a different perspective. We invite you to consider the idea, that by taking 'editorial control' of your own conversations about food (the ones inside your head), you become a *conscious consumer* and start eating and drinking consciously, as an act of self-love that is nourishing to every aspect of self.

Nourishing ourselves from an integrated perspective, means making conscious choices, not just about what we eat and drink but also when and where. Perhaps above all, it is about being conscious of why we eat and drink because once we get that part straight, all the rest of it seems to fall into place.

Why do you eat, is it to nourish your body? Do you drink in order to hydrate your body? Or is it to fill a physical or emotional void? If you're not sure why you consume whatever it is that you consume, all you need to do is to ask and to be honest with yourself when you answer. And if you're wondering what to do if you don't get an answer, you simply do what you would do for anybody that you love and keep asking. We don't always eat or drink for the same reasons and being a conscious consumer means being aware of the reasons behind the choices we make. This in turn enables us to make informed choices about how we nourish ourselves. It's not about being self-critical or judgmental, it's about being genuinely curious and honest with ourselves about how and why we eat and drink.

The conversations we have with ourselves about food are some of the most important conversations we will ever have because the choices we make about what we consume are so crucial to our well-being. In 400 B.C. the Greek physician Hippocrates, the undisputed father of modern medicine told us straight, that food is the key to good health and well-being and also that the solutions to our health problems are to be found in food. He noticed that the food we eat can enable us to maintain mental and physical well-being and also help to prevent illness as well as to treat illness and regain health. In other words, he was advising us to use food not only to stay well through a balanced diet, but also to become well again when things go wrong. In Hippocrates' Greece and across all of Europe and Asia, in the rainforests of central and South America and on every other continent on Earth, food has been used to intentionally affect health, both as a preventative and as a remedy since ancient times. There are endless examples of everyday ingredients that are used as natural remedies; from garlic as a cure for fungal infections, to yoghurt for sunburn relief; fermented vegetables as a natural probiotic and cider vinegar as a remedy for just about anything.

When it comes to our everyday nutrition, science has taught us much about how food interacts with our bodies to produce energy and how complex and utterly miraculous that process is. Metabolism, which is the transfer of food and oxygen into heat and water by the body to create energy, was discovered in the 1700's. In the 1800's, the elements of carbon, nitrogen, hydrogen, and oxygen, were identified as the main components of food. A hundred years or so later, a Polish doctor called Casimir Funk identified what he called 'vitamins' as essential to the human diet.

Today, nutritional science is a vast and complex subject that encompasses the effects and interactions of different foods and food groups, food production and processing methods and diet patterns. It covers everything about the food we eat and the way our body processes it, from the best dietary composition for weight loss and gain, to the interaction of prebiotics and probiotics, fermented food and gut microbiota, as well as the effects of fatty acids, flavonoids, and other bioactives. The more we learn, the more we realise the complexity of it. This is only to be expected given recent advances in nutritional science and the fact that an increase in complexity is always evident wherever there is scientific progress, from nutrition and medicine, to physics and economics. Initial observations lead us to reasonable assumptions and theories that achieve practical benefits, until they are inevitably outdated and often contradicted, by new knowledge and the recognition of ever-increasing complexity.

Nevertheless, we have known for thousands of years what is and is not good for us. We've known why for nearly three hundred years and by now we should all be rather good at eating foods that are beneficial and avoiding those that are not. But that's not what the statistics suggest. To cut a long and well-researched story short, at least in the west and increasingly in the east, we have never been so fat or greedy. It sounds harsh but it's the bitter truth.

"If you keep good food in your fridge,
you will eat good food."
-
Erick McAdams

Food is a fundamentally important feature in our lives. It really is one of life's great pleasures, but we are often too busy feeling guilty about what we eat and drink, or just too busy to really savour what we consume. Or worse still, we don't enjoy food at all and only eat to stay alive. When we begin to think about not just what but *why* and *when* we eat, it's easy to see how habits like snacking shortly before bed, or stuffing a mass-produced sandwich down your throat as quickly as possible while standing on a packed train and reading a book, is not conscious eating and is unlikely to be good for you. We also use food as a reward and as a way of comforting ourselves and also, as a way of punishing ourselves. We get emotional about food and sometimes irrational, which is why simple advice like emptying the kitchen cupboards and fridge of all the things we find difficult to resist (unless we are happy to keep eating them), is very good advice for those who want to have more control over their consumption. In the absence of health issues or allergies, the best advice to the average person seems to have changed very little over the years; eat a diverse range of fresh, local, preferably organic, mainly plant-based, produce in a variety of textures, covering all the colours of the rainbow, across all food groups and listen to how your body reacts to what you put in it. But we're not here to give you advice about *what* to eat and instead encourage you to focus on the *why* and make it a habit to be a conscious consumer, who is aware of and in control of what, when, how and *why* you eat and drink.

How we eat and drink is absolutely foundational to our well-being but too many of us treat our bodies more like a waste disposal unit than a sacred temple. There are some who see the food we eat as the bricks and mortar of who we are. They say that every morsel we consume has a direct impact on every cell in our body and that we alter our very DNA each time we eat. They believe we are *literally* what we eat. We don't know if this is a biological fact but even in the absence of proof, wouldn't it be a good thing if all our decisions about food were based on the assumption that it is?

REALISATION PRACTICE: *Wish I Hadn't List*

We've all heard of 'wish lists', and we all love making them! Now, you're going to make two wish lists to help you seize control of what you consume and take back sovereignty over what you put in your body; a *Wish I Hadn't* and a *Wish I Had list.*

- For seven days make a note of everything you consume that you *Wish I Hadn't.*

- Review and create a *Wish I Had* list of healthy alternatives.
- Physically remove from your fridge and cupboards all items of food and drink that are on your *Wish I Hadn't* list and replace them with the healthy alternatives on your *Wish I Had* list.
- For the next seven days, observe yourself as you adhere to the healthy options on your *Wish I Had* list and reflect on the following questions:
  > *What's different about your inner dialogue?*
  > *How does that make you feel?*
  > *What will you choose to do from now when it comes to what you wish for?*

MIRROR MOMENT: *The Food of Love*

Imagine that you are responsible for the nutrition of somebody who you love unconditionally, whom you hold in the highest regard and whose current and future health and well-being are paramount. What are the main considerations that you take into account as you consider what to feed them? Now reflect on how this compares to the choices you make in relation to your own diet.

FITNESS

"Those who think they have no time for exercise will sooner or later have to find time for illness."

-

Edward Stanley

Centuries ago, Western culture lost sight of the interconnectedness between the body, the mind and spirit, and how each has the power to affect the other. Cultivating a love of movement can help you get beyond the concept of physical fitness as separate from cognitive, emotional and spiritual fitness.

If you already love swimming, jogging, tap dancing, going to the gym, have just completed your latest marathon or own a mountain bike that's been out of the shed at least once a week in the last year, you may think that you can skip or whizz through this section, but there's a lot more to it than that. Here's some food for thought and reflection around what it means to be fit.

Being physically fit is not just about exercise, any physical activity is an excellent way to reduce stress and promote well-being. This is because, among other things, physical activity helps to dispel the hormones produced during the stress response, allowing the body to normalise.

Lack of time is the predominant reason people give for not keeping fit. But the truth is, the most common obstacle is a lack of personal commitment. Making a personal choice not to focus on physical health and well-being.

People who exercise regularly do so for two basic reasons; either because they enjoy exercising, or because they enjoy the benefits of exercising, or a combination of both.

What would it take for you to take it to the next level, whether that means starting to exercise, starting to exercise more, or starting to enjoy it more?

If you find it difficult to fit extended periods of exercise into your schedule, keep in mind that even short bouts of physical activity in 10-minute segments, can still help you achieve health benefits.

And you don't need a gym in the basement or a mountain bike in the shed or indeed a mountain to climb. Making a start to bringing the many benefits of physical movement and regular exercise into your life, can be as simple as making the decision to start walking up and down the stairs instead of taking the elevator.

One thing that often gets overlooked when it comes to our physical well-being is the quality of our breathing. Are you a nose-breather, a mouth-breather or both? Studies show that breathing through the nose has many more benefits, although, when exercising, mouth breathing can help get oxygen to your muscles faster.

It turns out that breathing is a lot more complicated than it looks. The nose produces nitric oxide, which improves the ability of our lungs to absorb oxygen and increases the transportation of oxygen throughout the body, including the heart. Nitric oxide is also antifungal, antiviral, antiparasitic and antibacterial, which helps the immune system fight infection. Other advantages include:

- The nose adds moisture to the air to prevent dryness in the lungs and bronchial tubes.
- The nose warms up cold air to body temperature before it gets to your lungs.
- Nose breathing also adds resistance to the air stream, which increases oxygen uptake by maintaining the lungs elasticity.

Many studies have also shown that a longer exhale than inhale is a great way to combat fight-or-flight stress responses and improve overall health and cognition. We have something called a *sympathetic nervous system* and when we breathe in, it accelerates our heart rate and when we breathe out, there is a deceleration caused by our *parasympathetic nervous system.*

So being fit is just as much about becoming conscious of our breathing and mindful of our movement, as it is about sweating it out at the gym.

REALISATION PRACTICE: *Keeping it F.I.T!*

One of the most powerful things you can do is to change how you think about physical activity and become more mindful of your movement. The next time you exercise, or enter into any kind of physical activity, the first and most important thing to do is to be aware of what you're doing and how you're doing it. Instead of distracting yourself with television, social media and unrelated thoughts, focus your attention on your physical sensations, on your breathing and the movement of your body. Give your full attention to your chosen activity and you will do it more effectively and also avoid unnecessary injury.

Here's an easy way to keep fit and stay safe with *F.I.T.*

Frequency – Become aware of how often you exercise and how much time you spend doing it. The body goes through a process of rebuild and repair to replenish the energy reserves consumed by our chosen exercise or activity. The frequency needs to be a balance between providing just enough stress for the body to adapt and allowing enough time for healing and adaptation to occur.

Intensity – Become aware of how much you push yourself and the intensity of your exercise or activity. Intensity is about being conscious of the amount of effort that is being invested in an activity at any given time.

Technique – Become aware of how you do what you do. Regardless of what you choose: running, walking, swimming, dancing, cycling, aerobics, tennis, circuit training, trampolining; be conscious of the best technique to get the most benefit from the activity and avoid injury.

MIRROR MOMENT: *Am I fit?*

Take a moment to reflect and do a quick rating on a scale of 1-5 (5 is high) in relation to how satisfied you are with the quality of your:

- Strength
- Stamina
- Flexibility
- Breathing

What will you do to improve your lowest scores?

REST

"If you get tired, learn to rest not to quit."

-

Banksy

As already mentioned, stress has a huge impact on our health and our ability to get well and be well and knowing how to manage our own stress levels by knowing how to 'wind down' and get enough rest and enough sleep, is vital to our well-being.

Rest is defined as what we do to let stress go during the day, at the end of the day, at the end of the week and whenever we go on holiday. As the old adage goes, 'a change is as good as a rest' and when we're on holiday, we're away from the stresses of everyday life. Leisure time, doing things that we find pleasurable and having fun, is also vital for resting our mind and body and compensating for a stressful job or responsibilities at home. For some of us that means a hobby or interest that we feel passionate about, meeting up with friends, baking, exercising, reading a good book or watching a film that we can immerse ourselves in.

Feeling rested, being able to stay calm under pressure and manage our stress levels, is also dependent on how much good quality sleep we get. Do you feel that you got enough quality sleep last night? The National Sleep Foundation says an average of eight hours of sleep per night is the ideal for adults and yet studies show two-thirds of us sleep less than that. According to neuroscientist and author of, *Why We Sleep,* Mark O'Connell, this is symptomatic of a 'silent sleep loss epidemic' and he warns that routinely sleeping less than six or seven hours a night demolishes our immune system and more than doubles our risk of cancer.

Whether or not we heed the advice of sleep experts, we all know that sleep is important and that the quality and quantity of our sleep impacts both how we feel and what we can achieve. Even without fully understanding the nature of sleep, we know that going without sleep makes us feel terrible, while getting a good night's sleep can change everything and make us feel ready for anything. It's not at all surprising that we find it more difficult to take in new information after a night of disturbed sleep. What is surprising is that it's equally important to get a good night's sleep after learning something new in order to process and retain the information that's been absorbed. Not only do we decline in terms of function when we don't get enough quality sleep, it can also lead to long-term health issues. That's why if we're having sleep problems, it's important that we recognise it and confront these difficulties before discomfort turns to disease. Studies have shown that sleep plays a critical role in immune function, metabolism, memory, learning and other vital functions. The constant disruption of our body clock or circadian rhythm through night shift work and frequent travelling across time zones, can be severely detrimental to our health and has been linked to obesity, type 2 diabetes, depression, peptic ulcers, heart disease and cancer. Sleep isn't a luxury, it's a necessity and it really matters. It also matters how much of our sleep time we spend dreaming, which is connected to how much stress we experience during the day.

What's the purpose of our dreams? One of the founders of the *human givens* school of psychology, Joe Griffin, was the first person to review all the available scientific data and conduct research that resulted in the discovery of a theory about why we dream.

This has helped transform our understanding of consciousness and explain many previously mysterious phenomena of the human psyche, including the symptoms of depression, psychosis, and hypnotic states. We learned that dreams are metaphorical translations of waking expectations. This is important because expectations that cause strong emotions that are not acted upon during the day, are metaphorically played out in dreams. This enables us to deactivate them and resolve things in our dreams, which frees up the brain to respond afresh to each new day.

For the average person, dreams take up about a third of the time that we're asleep and the remainder of the time is when we completely shut down and fully rest in deep sleep. This is why dreaming too much can be a problem and prevent us from getting enough quality rest. One of the main functions of dreaming is to resolve concerns and problems, largely from that day and unresolved past events. This could explain reoccurring dreams. The more stressed we are, the more we dream and the less restful sleep we have. This is why when we are going through a stressful time, we can sometimes wake up feeling more tired and less rested than we did when we went to bed.

Here are some good practices for improving your chances of getting a good night's sleep:

- Quieten your mind by downloading your priorities and concerns; before you switch off your technology, make a note of any concerns, challenges or issues you want to return to and create a to-do list.
- Switch off anything with a screen two hours before bedtime.
- Don't take your phone to bed, preferably leave it outside the room or at the very least put it on flight mode and keep it at arms-length.
- Stop consuming solids two hours before bedtime.
- Stop all consumption of sugar, caffeine and alcohol four hours before bedtime.
- Keep a notebook and pencil beside your bed and make a note of any stray thoughts or concerns as soon as they arise and then close your notebook… physically and metaphorically.
- Find your favourite way of winding down for two hours before bed; read or tell a story; listen to or make music, have or give a massage; have a bath alone or with that special someone; create intimacy with your words or actions.
- Add your own ideas to this list as you become more aware of how to promote a good night's sleep.

REALISATION PRACTICE: *Dream Catcher*

Dream analysis has always been a crucial way of looking into your subconscious and gaining insights about who you truly are, but many people either don't remember their dreams at all, or have a hazy recollection of them on waking that fades some time before breakfast. If you are one of those people, the good news is that you can learn how to remember your dream in order to be able to tap into important self-knowledge.

This exercise works well if you have good mental health, but if you're anxious or depressed, it can actually deepen that anxiety or depression as it can interfere with what the brain is trying to process subconsciously. If you're in any doubt, our advice is to skip this practice until you're feeling stronger.

To train yourself to remember your dreams you need to get into the habit of making a note of them as soon as you awake. To do this, have a pen and paper next to the bed and make a note of whatever you remember when you awake this can be anything from a keyword to a few sentences.

First ask yourself what if anything your dreams tell you literally or metaphorically, about yourself?

Then, ask yourself what your *analysis* of your dreams tells you about yourself?

MIRROR MOMENT: *Rest Easy*

Getting rest means different things to different people, how do you get your rest? Make a list of everything you did in the last 48 hours that you would describe as restful. As you reflect on your list, what do you notice? Is there anything you need to do differently?

SELF-ASSESSMENT

- When it comes to my physical well-being (PQ), where am I doing well?
- Where is there room for improvement?
- What do I want to work on?
- Where do I want to focus primarily?
- On a scale of 1-10 (10 is high) how satisfied am I with the level of my current, overall physical well-being?

SELF-COACHING: What would love do?

In Chapter Two we introduced you to our love-based coaching model and now you get to put it into practice in relation to your physical well-being. You will probably have identified one or more areas where you can improve. Choose which of these you want to start with and write a short opening statement that best describes it as the topic you want to focus on, as if you were going to share it with a coach. E.g. *I know my posture isn't good, but I don't know what to do about it.* You can then repeat this process for each of the areas you want to work on.

STEP 1: What would love ask?

Imagine it's a loved one and not yourself that you're talking to and that it's *their* topic. If the aim of this step is to know what the 'other person' wants, what question/s do you want to ask in order to understand? And how would you answer each of those question/s?

STEP 2: What would love say?

Imagine it's a loved one and not yourself that you're talking to and it's *their* answer/s, what would you say in response and how would you say it?

STEP 3: What would love do?

Imagine it's a loved one and not yourself that you're talking to and it's *their* topic you are offering advice on, what would you advise them to do?

STEP 4: What stops you?

Based on this inner dialogue, what stops you from taking your own advice and acting from a place of self-love? If nothing is stopping you, then all you need to do is take action. *If something is stopping you, go back to Step 1 and repeat the cycle – but focus on your answer to this question – until you know what to do, how and when to do it and there's nothing else stopping you.*

COGNITIVE

"Intelligence is the ability to learn
from experience, adapt to new situations,
understand and handle abstract concepts."

-

R. J. Sternberg

The way we define cognitive intelligence or IQ is through four major elements: *Present Awareness, Perspective Shifting, Intention* and *Learning Agility.*

PRESENT AWARENESS – mindfulness, beginner's mind, clarity
PERSPECTIVE SHIFTING – exploring and modelling new realities
MAGICAL THINKING – harnessing the power of intention and imagination
LEARNING AGILITY – learning how to learn and being ready for anything

Present Awareness includes mindfulness, which is the ability to step outside of our thinking and observe with clarity. Beginner's mind is when we let go of being the expert, so we can listen to others with an open mind or look at situations through new eyes. Having a beginner's mind enables us to keep learning by seeing new opportunities and new realities.

Once we see these new perspectives, *perspective shifting* is the ability to think, feel and act in line with them, so that we model and then benefit from new realities.

Magical thinking is what happens when we reclaim sovereignty over our minds and consciously align two of the greatest powers on Earth: The creative power of our imagination and the operational power of our intention. This is our software, literally the basic operating system of every human being and it has no limitations. It can make anything happen.

One of the hallmarks for cognitive well-being is *learning agility*, which means being good at picking up new things as you go along in life. We are learning agile when our thoughts, feelings and behaviour are adaptable, resilient and innovative. This is really important because it is this ability to learn, change and adapt to the environment, that enables us to thrive in any circumstances. It is absolutely key to creativity and innovative thinking, to inspirational leadership and to exceptional performance and results in whatever you do.

PRESENT AWARENESS

> "Success depends on the quality of attention and intention that an individual brings to any situation."
>
> -
>
> *Otto Scharmer (paraphrased)*

We have a natural ability to step outside of our conditioning. When this 'observing self' is activated, either through mindfulness or other kinds of meditation, we step back from our conditioned self and widen the focus of our attention so that we can see and question ourselves from multiple viewpoints. This observing self is a more fundamental part of who we are, even more than our thinking and feeling. The '*I am*' before we are anything else.

I am a man... I am a teacher... I am happy... I am sad.

We believe there is a universal *I am* that we all share and which is the natural state that unites us all in the 'oneness' of life. It is the basis of many of the world's spiritual traditions. There are many benefits to moving into this state that have a profound effect on our experience of life.

"If a pond is clouded with mud, there's nothing you can do to make the water clear. But when you allow the mud to settle, it will clear on its own, because clarity is the water's natural state... Clarity is your mind's natural state."

-

Jamie Smart

This universal resource that Jamie is talking about has been 'covered up' by what he calls contaminated thinking. As people allow their mud to settle, clarity emerges and they discover they have what they need for the job at hand, also known as a 'flow' state.

All great sports players, musicians, actors, public speakers, leaders etc., would agree that the key to success is to be in 'flow'. To clear the mind, be in the moment, and do what is needed.

"Awareness is the power that is concealed within the present moment. This is why we may also call it Presence."

-

Eckhart Tolle

Most of the time, most of us live in a daydream in which we mull over the past and either fear for or dream of the future. Meanwhile life proceeds without us. We think of meditating or being mindful as something you do while sitting, legs crossed, eyes closed, completely clearing the mind... but actually, it's about being mindful of being in *present awareness*. Being so fully present, that you are a part of the moment rather than lost in your head, somewhere in the past or the future.

Mindfulness and meditation have both been shown to have physical and mental health benefits and there is often confusion about what they are. Meditation leads to many different things, including mindful awareness, but you don't have to sit in a meditative state to become mindful. You can practice being mindful anywhere, anytime, anyhow and whether or not you are alone or with others.

The cultivation of moment-to-moment awareness of our current surroundings is a simple and potentially life-changing practice, that helps us better cope with the difficult thoughts and feelings that cause us stress and anxiety in everyday life.

The practice of awareness of the present moment enables us to disassociate with notions of past and future that trigger rumination and stress. Through mindful breathing meditation, we use the breath as an object of meditation, concentrating deeply on the rhythm and sensation of our most basic life force. Think of it as an exercise for your brain that strengthens your 'attention muscle' by forcing your awareness inward and challenging you to stay focused.

In perhaps the most significant and fascinating mindfulness study to date, a team of Harvard researchers found that after eight weeks of daily practice, mindful meditators reported a sense of increased peace and clarity, while non-meditators did not. Not only that, but their MRIs showed an increase in grey matter in parts of the brain associated with focus and attention and a decrease in grey matter associated with stress and anxiety (non-meditators remained unchanged).

Like any other practice, such as physical exercise or healthy eating, you have to adapt things to work for you. Mindfulness is just the same. There is no 'one size fits all'.

However you choose to do it, with the regular practice of mindfulness exercises, we take ourselves off auto-pilot and cease to be blindly led by emotions that are steeped in negative past experiences or fear of the future. We harness our natural ability to root the mind in the present moment and can deal with life's challenges in ways that are clear-headed, calm and assertive.

In turn, we develop a fully conscious mind-set that frees us from the imprisonment of unhelpful, self-limiting thought patterns. This allows us to be fully present and consciously aware of the positive emotions that increase our compassion and understanding of self and others.

In addition to what goes on inside our heads, we also face the many external distractions of our busy world. We fold the laundry while keeping one eye on the kids and another on the television. We plan our day while listening to the radio and commuting to work and then plan the weekend on the way back, while writing that report. And in the midst of all the 'doing', we lose our connection with the present moment and miss out on just 'being' human *beings*. Do you remember whether or not you felt well-rested this morning? Did you notice if the forsythia bush that you see every day on your way to work is in bloom yet? Can you recall everything you've had to eat and drink since this time yesterday?

When we are mindful, we are more likely to have attitudes and habits that lead to a more satisfying experience of life. Being mindful makes us more present and able to enjoy life's pleasures, as well as to cope better when things go wrong. The timeless sense of being in *flow* or in the zone, is another of the many benefits and rewards of mindfulness. There's less regret and rumination over the past, less worry and concern about the future, less pre-occupation with notions of success and failure and less looking sideways and comparison to others favourable or otherwise.

Mindfulness improves physical health. Scientists have discovered that mindfulness techniques help improve physical health in a number of ways. Mindfulness can help relieve stress, treat heart disease, lower blood pressure, reduce chronic pain, improve sleep and alleviate digestive problems.

Mindfulness improves mental health. In recent years, psychotherapists have turned to mindfulness meditation as an important element in the treatment of a number of problems including: Depression, substance abuse, eating disorders, couples' conflicts, anxiety disorders and obsessive-compulsive disorder.

Mindfulness improves emotional health. Mindfulness is the practice of purposely focusing your attention on the present moment- while accepting it without judgment. Mindfulness is now being examined scientifically and has been found to be a key element in stress reduction and overall happiness. Professor emeritus Jon Kabat-Zinn, founder and former director of the Stress Reduction Clinic at the University of Massachusetts Medical Center, helped to bring the practice of mindfulness meditation into mainstream medicine. He demonstrated that practicing mindfulness can bring improvements in both physical and psychological symptoms, as well as positive changes in health, attitudes, and behaviours.

Mindfulness improves spiritual health. The cultivation of mindfulness has roots in Buddhism, but most spiritual traditions and religions include some type of prayer or meditation technique that helps shift your thoughts away from your usual preoccupations. A shift toward an appreciation of the moment and a bigger perspective on life.

REALISATION PRACTICE: *Mindfulness*

Choose any or all of the following practices to become more presently aware.

Mindful Breathing

You can do this anywhere, any time and in any position. Wherever you are, get comfortable, relax your body as much as you can, be still and focus on your breath for one minute. Start by breathing slowly in and out. One cycle of breath should last for about seven seconds. Breathe in through your nose and out through your mouth, letting your breath flow smoothly in and out of your body. Let go of your thoughts and all the things you have to do next. Be conscious of your thoughts and don't try to fight or get rid of them. Simply allow them to come and go while you stay focused on your breath. If you enjoy the first minute of conscious breathing, you can continue for as many more minutes as you like.

Mindful Immersion

This practice is designed to cultivate a heightened awareness, appreciation of everyday tasks and the results they achieve. Think of something mundane that you do more than once every day and that you rarely, if ever, notice when you're doing it. Something like opening a door, filling the kettle or pouring a glass of water. At the very moment you touch the doorknob to open the door, or turn on the tap or take the glass from the cupboard, stop and become mindful of where you are, how you are feeling in the moment and where the door leads to, or how the tea or water will refresh and hydrate you.

Make it your intention to practice mindful immersion whenever you remember and see an opportunity. You can extend mindful immersion beyond the physical to become intentional about your thoughts and feelings too. For example, every time you catch yourself having a negative thought, you can take a moment to notice it, label it as unhelpful and choose to let it go or replace it with a different perspective.

Mindful Walking
In this practice you just start walking. It doesn't matter where you're going, in fact it's better if you don't know where you are headed because mindfulness is all about process rather than outcome.

As you walk, pay attention to your breathing and to how your body feels. Notice physical sensations like wind or rain against your skin, or the leaves beneath your feet. Notice what you can hear and see around you. Be aware of all the colours. The aim is to have the experience of hearing and seeing without labelling or judging what you hear and see. Allow your thoughts to come and go and consciously shift your attention back to the sensation of being fully present and aware.

MIRROR MOMENT: *Watch the Watcher*

Here's an interesting practice of self-observation. As you are reading these words, become aware of yourself reading and of your reaction to these words. What are you thinking, what are you feeling, as you read? Now observe yourself as the person having those thoughts and feelings. In other words, watch the watcher.

"What we are looking for is what is looking."

-

St. Francis of Assisi

Now try watching the watcher with something else. Choose an object to observe and then divide your awareness in two so that you are looking at the object, while at the same time observing yourself looking at the object. Observe this for as long as you can.

Don't worry if you become distracted by random thoughts, this is quite normal in meditative practice to begin with. Just accept it and keep returning your attention to the object you are observing and then you as the observer.

PERSPECTIVE SHIFTING

"If you change the way you look at things,
the things you look at change."

-

Dr. Wayne Dyer

Experience is not formed by what happens to you, it's formed by how you interpret what happens. And because everybody experiences, understands and interprets the world differently, everybody's representation of reality is unique. Reality as we perceive it depends on how we process information from our surroundings and this in turn depends on our personal needs, values, attitudes, beliefs, language and a whole host of other things, including what we have experienced in the past. So, we form beliefs and stories about what is and is not true, by processing information from the world around us through all these filters. This colours our experience, which in turn reinforces our stories and beliefs, which in turn colours our perception. Perception is a very dynamic, largely unconscious and self-perpetuating process of selection, focus, interpretation, explanation and organisation of information. It's a process that's unique to each individual and it's based on what we perceive to be true, as a result of our needs, wants, values, fears and experiences.

In a simple example, an individual may have had a bad experience that leads them to believe that the world is full of people that can't be trusted. They may then spend years or even a whole lifetime reinforcing this perspective or 'map of the world', even though they have long forgotten how it was formed in the first place. This is how belief becomes 'fact' and personal perspective becomes 'reality'.

Your mind is your 'map of the world'. It's the way you perceive yourself, the world and everything and everyone you encounter. But the map is not the territory. Like a map, it's just a representation of the territory and if you find that you are not going in the direction you would like or getting the results you would prefer, then all you need to do is change your map!

This is not as difficult or complicated as it sounds and in fact there are just a few simple steps to achieving this. The first and by far the most important step, is to become aware of your thoughts and notice how positive or negative they are. What do you tell yourself when you're not paying attention? Are you one of the majority of people on the planet who make thousands of negative remarks to themselves and about themselves every day? And if you are, how much of it is repetition?

We are all aware of the power of repetition, it's how people are brainwashed. So it's easy to understand how important it is to do something about the contents of your head. You would never talk to anyone else the way that you talk to yourself, you would never say out loud the things that you hear inside your own mind. You may have thought there was no escape from this inner tyrant, but now you know better. The cavalry is here and it's you in the saddle! You and only you have the power to overcome the darkness in your head. This is how you take action. Insight and awareness is nothing without action. You cannot have, do and be everything you want, if you don't take action and the first action you need to take is to control your thinking.

To control your thinking begin by recognising the distinction between you and your mind. Remember, *you are not your mind.* You are not the thought. You are the one who *has* the thought. As soon as you are able to watch or witness a thought, you are one step removed from it and you can see it for what it is… just a thought. You can also see the interrelationship between your thoughts, feelings and behaviours and how *where the mind goes, the body follows.*

The placebo effect is a great example of mind over matter and thanks to recent advances in brain science, we now understand how it works, which makes it no less miraculous and even more compelling as something we can harness and leverage as a life skill.

In his book, *You Are the Placebo,* Dr. Joe Dispenza cites many documented cases of people who have cured themselves of serious, chronic disease, including cancer, heart disease, depression and Parkinson's disease, through the power of belief in a placebo. There are also countless documented cases of the opposite effect where people were misdiagnosed with something that later showed up in their body. In some cultures, the power of belief is so strong that people are taken ill and even die after being cursed.

This placebo effect happens when thoughts are stronger and more real than the outside world and the brain and body can't tell the difference between what is and is not 'real'.

Looking at the positive potential, this means you can harness the power of belief and use your imagination to transform your body, produce actual epigenetic changes and a whole new physical reality.

The key to creating your reality is to use a combination of clear intention and a strong feeling or emotion, to persuade your body that what you are imagining has already happened.

What's actually happening here is beyond the time and space of the third dimension, in the quantum *field of potential,* where the potential you selected through your intention has already happened. If you don't fully understand how this works, don't worry because few people do and it still does!

REALISATION PRACTICE: *Spot the Lighthouse*

This is purportedly the transcript of a radio conversation between a US naval ship and the Canadian authorities off the coast of Newfoundland in October, 1995.

AMERICANS: Please divert your course 15 degrees to the North to avoid a collision.
CANADIANS: Recommend you divert YOUR course 15 degrees to the South to avoid a collision.
AMERICANS: This is the Captain of a US Navy ship. I say again, divert YOUR course.

CANADIANS: No. I say again, you divert YOUR course.
AMERICANS: This is the aircraft carrier USS Lincoln, the second largest ship in the United States' Atlantic fleet. We are accompanied by three destroyers, three cruisers and numerous support vessels. I demand that YOU change your course 15 degrees north, that's one five degrees north, or countermeasures will be undertaken to ensure the safety of this ship.
CANADIANS: This is a lighthouse. Your call.

We really wanted this story to be true and suffice to say, it isn't. It seems the story has adapted and changed many times and according to some, its roots trace back to a simple joke above an animation in a 1930s cartoon sketch that reads… *Skipper: Where are you going with your blinking ship?* The Other: *"This isn't a blinking ship. It's a lighthouse!"* And, irrespective of provenance and veracity, it really lands the point that perspective changes everything.

Self-coaching questions to help you spot your 'lighthouses':

- Reflect on a situation in your life you're not fully satisfied with and would like to change.
- Make a list of things you can't change in relation to the situation.
- Make a list of things that you can change in relation to the situation.
- What would be different if you chose to spend your time and energy on what you can do?

Consciously reduce the time and energy you spend on what you can't change and intentionally focus your time and energy on what you can.

MIRROR MOMENT: *Limiting Limiting Beliefs*

Listen to inner dialogue as you answer the following questions. What do you learn about beliefs you hold that may no longer serve you?

- What limiting belief do you hold about yourself and how would you benefit if you changed it?
- What limiting belief do you hold about someone else and how would you benefit if you changed it?
- What limiting belief do you hold about life and how would you benefit if you changed it?

Now you know what's in it for you, why wouldn't you limit your limiting beliefs?

Your answer to this last question could be one of the key limiting beliefs that you hold, that prevent you from getting well, being well and doing well in life!

MAGICAL THINKING

"Everything that happens in the universe begins with intention."

-

Deepak Chopra

If you look up the definition of magical thinking, you'll find a number of different perspectives. From psychiatry, which defines magical thinking as a disorder of thought content; through psychology, which focuses more on how having the belief that thought creates or that thinking is the same as doing, can cause or fuel fear and anxiety; to anthropology, which denotes magical thinking as the attribution of causality between groups. In any case, the relationship between cause and effect is the common denominator.

For our purposes, when we talk about magical thinking, we're using the term magic in perhaps it's purest sense. At the very root of the word is an old persian word, *magush,* meaning *'to be able, to have power'*. So, for us, *magical thinking* is about being aware of and in control of our thoughts as the architect of our reality.

We considered calling this section *Brain Power* because ultimately, that's what *magical thinking* is. It's having power over our brain and using that power to cause a desired effect. This happens through a combination of *imagination, intention and influence* in a creative dance that goes something like this; the mind has a thought at the level of vibration. When this vibration meets emotion it becomes energy and this energy *in motion* then influences the possibilities in the field of potential, where it becomes matter.

We can find sound scientific reasons for this, grounded in the world of quantum physics. In his book *Wholeness and Implicate Order,* scientist, David Bohm, suggests that all ordering, influence and information is present in an invisible space or domain – a higher reality – that we can 'call upon'.

In her book, The Field, Lynne McTaggart describes a field of potential called the Zero Point Field, for which there is an extraordinary body of evidence from scientists all over the world. She explains in detail how the field is a living entity, a life force, which is responsible for many of the most profound mysteries of our existence, *"Einstein himself believed space constituted a true void until his own ideas, eventually developed into his general theory of relativity, showed that space indeed held a plenum of activity.* But it *wasn't until 1911, with an experiment by Max Planck, one of the founding fathers of quantum theory, that physicists understood that empty space was bursting with activity*".

The existence of a vast sea of infinite possibility and potential has unfathomable implications for us as individuals and humanity as a whole. The theory that all matter everywhere is interconnected by waves, spread out across time and space to infinity, offers scientific explanation and credence to many metaphysical concepts. It reduces the chasm between science and spirituality by offering an explanation for the existence of ch'i, the life force at the centre of Eastern spiritual practice that runs through everything; the biblical notion that God imagined the world into matter from energy or light. Our aim is not to persuade you of the existence of this field of potential and for further proof or evidence, highly recommend that you read *The Field.* We want to focus instead on how we can access and use it to cause the desired effect.

In physics, a field is described as a matrix or medium which connects two or more points in space by a physical force like electromagnetism or gravity. A force is represented as some kind of ripple or wave that enters and disrupts the activity in the field and does something. Simply put, the force is the *intention* and the field is a region of *influence. Imagination* is the vibration, the thought. Intention is the movement of that vibration into energy, which is made real or manifest due to the influence this exerts on infinite possibility. That is the basic nature of the field of potential. This is of course a gross simplification of the complex mechanics of reality creation and here's a simple model that makes it even easier to grasp…

I > IMAGINATION – an idea or vibration
I > INTENTION – movement of vibration into energy
I > INFLUENCE – energy influences possibility in the field of potential

REALISATION PRACTICE: *Creating a Vision Board*

It's easy to dismiss the idea of creating a vision board as a bit silly or 'arts and crafts' but it can be a very powerful way of putting the above model into practice by capturing your imagination. A vision board provides inspiration and physical evidence of your intention, identifying and influencing your dreams and keeping you focused and motivated in relation to what you really want in life.

Collect inspirational images for your vision board. You want it to be fun and engaging, to contain plenty of words and images that you find appealing and that demand your focus and attention.

Place your vision board where you will see it every day. Your goal in making this vision board, is to create a reminder of what you are intending to accomplish and to put it in clear view to inspire you and help maintain your focus and attention on turning your vision into reality.

MIRROR MOMENT: *Brain Power*

Listen to your inner dialogue in this moment as you answer the following questions…

- How much brain power do you spend thinking about the past?
- How much brain power do you spend thinking about the future?
- How much brain power do you spend in the present moment?
- How much brain power do you spend thinking creatively?

- How much brain power do you spend thinking logically?
- How much brain power do you spend reacting emotionally to life?

Are you happy with where you spend your brain power and if not, what are you going to do about it?

LEARNING AGILITY

"It's no use going back to yesterday,
because I was a different person then."
-
Lewis Carroll

In an ever changing world, where anything can happen and nothing is certain, it becomes essential to remain open to new ways of thinking and to be willing and able to continuously adapt what we do and how we do it.

Learning agility is about having the will and ability to learn from an experience and to apply that learning the next time you do something. This requires that we apply everything we have talked about so far in relation to cognitive intelligence. *Present awareness* enables us to remain calm in the face of difficulty and observe the current situation with a clear head. We also need to plan ahead and this too benefits from being done in a state of present awareness. We can then calmly and clearly observe a situation, focus on the things we can change and accept the things we can't. It's really important to recognise that acceptance is not the same as agreement because it means we can strongly disagree and yet still accept the reality. This enables us to stop obsessing about things that are beyond our control and to instead focus our time and energy on the right things. *Perspective shifting* and *magical thinking* help us to see opportunities instead of the limitations and enable us to take the right action. This leads to different ways of doing things, new skills, greater resilience and an overall better experience of life.

The ability to continuously learn and adapt determines the extent to which we not only survive but thrive in turbulent times. We will always face new challenges and have issues. What separates the successful from those who struggle, is how they experience these challenges and what they take forward from the experience. It would serve us all well to be more learning agile. We can take more risks and challenge the status quo, while ensuring we are both in the present moment and reflective after the fact and we can choose not to be defensive in the face of disagreement or critisism. The extent to which we are able to do this will have an impact not only on who we are today, but also on who we can become tomorrow.

Learning agility is a mind-set that focuses on growth and potential. People who have it develop habits that allow them to continually grow and to create new strategies for increasingly complex lives.

Some of the habits that emerge from a learning agile mind-set include…

- Challenging the status quo
- Challenging self
- Asking for feedback
- Reflecting on experiences
- Reflecting on insights
- Asking for help when needed
- Progressive risk taking
- Calmness in adversity

REALISATION PRACTICE: *3As*

Choose something in your life that isn't working for you or that creates inner or outer conflict for you. Something that causes you stress and that you would like to relate to differently. Now answer the questions in the model, the aim of which is to empower you to shift from an unhealthy to a healthy perspective in relation to the topic.

A > AWARENESS – What do you need to be aware of?
A > ACCEPTANCE – What do you need to accept?
A > ACTION – What actions do you need to take?

MIRROR MOMENT: *Learning About Me*

Reflecting on the last 48 hours, what have I learned about myself?

SELF-ASSESSMENT

- When it comes to my cognitive well-being (IQ), where am I doing well?
- Where is there room for improvement?
- What do I want to work on?
- Where do I want to focus primarily?
- On a scale of 1-10 (10 is high) how satisfied am I with the level of my current, overall cognitive well-being?

SELF-COACHING: *What would love do?*

You will probably have identified one or more areas where you can improve your cognitive well-being. Choose which of these you want to start with and write a short opening statement that best describes it as the topic you want to focus on. E.g. *I know I need to let go, but I can't stop feeling resentful about how things turned out with my brother and my mother's will. You can then repeat this process for each of the areas you want to work on.*

STEP 1: What would love ask?

Imagine it's a loved one and not yourself that you're talking to and that it's their topic. If the aim of this step is to know what the 'other person' wants, what question/s do you want to ask in order to understand? And how would you answer each of those question/s?

STEP 2: What would love say?

Imagine it's a loved one and not yourself that you're talking to and it's their answer/s, what would you say in response and how would you say it?

STEP 3: What would love do?

Imagine it's a loved one and not yourself that you're talking to and it's their topic you are offering advice on, what would you advise them to do?

STEP 4: What stops you?

Based on this inner dialogue, what stops you from taking your own advice and acting from a place of self-love? If nothing is stopping you, then all you need to do is take action. If something is stopping you, go back to STEP 1 and repeat the cycle – focus on your answer to this question – until you know what to do, how and when to do it and there's nothing else stopping you.

EMOTIONAL

"Recognising, understanding, and choosing
how we think, feel, and act."

-

J. Freedman

The way we define emotional intelligence or EQ, is through four main elements: *Self-awareness, Self-regulation, Relationship Awareness* and *Relationship Skills.*

SELF-AWARENESS – understanding the relationship between thoughts, feelings and behaviours
SELF-REGULATION – managing thoughts, feelings and behaviours
RELATIONSHIP AWARENESS – understanding of other people's thoughts, feelings and behaviours
RELATIONSHIP SKILLS – building and maintaining effective relationships

We've all met brilliant people who are incredibly stupid, right? People who are limited by their narrow focus on brain power, logic and knowledge. People who think they can leave their emotions at the front door when they go to work in the morning and collect them on the way back. And we've all met people who left school at fifteen and now run a big global corporation, having climbed their way to the top from humble beginnings on the shop floor and who everyone describes as an inspiration.

The concept of Emotional Intelligence was developed by psychologists Peter Salovey and John Mayer, who described it as, '…the ability to perceive emotions, to access and generate emotions so as to assist thought, to understand emotions and emotional knowledge and to reflectively regulate emotions so as to promote emotional and intellectual growth'. Science journalist, Daniel Goleman, popularised it and most famously made a compelling and scientifically sound business case for emotional intelligence in the workplace, when he published Emotional Intelligence at Work in 1998. Many others have followed, all reaffirming his findings that *emotional intelligence counts for more than IQ or expertise in determining who will be a star-performer, whatever the job and that for outstanding leadership performance, it counts for almost everything.* One US study into what employers are looking for, found that the three most desired capabilities were communication skills, interpersonal skills and initiative. Harvard Business School lists empathy, perspective taking and rapport building, as what they look for in successful candidates, all of which are hallmarks of EQ.

EQ is more than just understanding emotions, it's about understanding the relationship between thoughts, feelings and behaviour in ourselves and in others. It is the ability to manage your own emotions and build and maintain healthy relationships and it is for this reason, that we have chosen to focus on four main aspects: *Self-awareness, Self-regulation, Relationship Awareness* and *Relationship Skills.*

Self-awareness is foundational to the others. We need to be aware of our thoughts and emotions and understand how they impact ourselves and others before we can have *Self-regulation,* which is the ability to control and manage our emotions and reactions. Not only must we understand ourselves, but also recognise that understanding others' thoughts, feelings and behaviours is also important – this is known as *Relationship Awareness.* Identifying a certain mood or emotion in others and consciously responding rather than reacting to it can go a long way in developing your *Relationship Skills,* which is the ability to build and maintain healthy relationships through the inevitable ups and downs.

SELF-AWARENESS

> "Until you make the unconscious conscious,
> it will direct your life and you will call it fate."
>
> –
>
> *C.G. Jung*

The ancient Greek aphorism 'Know Thyself' was the first of three maxims inscribed above the entrance to the Temple of Apollo at Delphi. And we believe it is not only the first competency you need to master emotional intelligence, it is also the first step in mastering your life. It is where you focus your attention, your emotions, reactions, personality and behaviour that determines your experience of life.

Self-awareness is about becoming acquainted with your inner thoughts and feelings and becoming conscious of what your brain tells you when you're not looking. Self-awareness is about understanding your inner world and being conscious of how this impacts your experience and intention. Self-awareness enables you to take control of your emotions, behaviour, and personality, so you can make the changes you want. Until you are aware, in the moment of your thoughts, emotions, words and behaviour, you will have difficulty making changes in the direction of your life. People with strong self-awareness are neither overly critical nor unrealistically hopeful. Rather they are honest with themselves and with others. They also recognise how their feelings affect them, other people and what they can achieve in life.

Having a clear understanding of your thought and behaviour patterns also helps you to understand other people and this ability to empathise facilitates better personal and professional relationships. When you can change your *interpretation* of what you experience, you can shift your emotions as well as the emotional quality of your relationships. When you can change the emotions in your relationships, you open up entirely new possibilities in life.

The hallmarks of self-awareness include self-confidence, realistic self-assessment and a light-hearted attitude that means we don't take ourselves too seriously. Self-awareness depends on our ability to monitor our own emotional state and impact. Someone with high self-awareness can clearly observe their inner dialogue and identify their personal belief systems, motivators, demotivators, strengths and weaknesses.

THE JOHARI WINDOW

The Johari Window is a great gizmo invented by two psychologists called Johan and Hari (...get it?) that helps us to increase our self-awareness through feedback and self-disclosure.

	Known by Self	Unknown by Self
Known by Others	OPEN	BLIND SPOT
Unknown by Others	HIDDEN	UNKNOWN

You can think of the window as a simple and effective tool or lens through which you can focus on the gap between your own perception of self and how others see you.

Quadrant 1 represents information about you that you are aware of and that others are also aware of. This quadrant is known as *open* and is generally where we find our comfort zone.

Quadrant 2 represents information about you that is known to others, but that you are unaware of. That's why this quadrant is described as our *blind spot.*

Quadrant 3 represents information about you that you are aware of but is hidden from others and hence the label of *hidden.*

Quadrant 4 represents information that neither you nor anyone else is aware of and is simply *unknown.*

Once you know all this, you can use it to become more self-aware. You can ask for feedback from others in order to reduce your blind spots, share information about yourself to reduce your hidden area and in this way consciously increase the size of your open quadrant.

Now here's a practice with which you can kick-start the process of increasing your self-awareness and get to know yourself a lot better.

REALISATION PRACTICE: *Quickie 360 Survey*

Choose 2-3 people and ask them to respond to the questions in the quick 360 Survey that follows, preferably in writing. If possible, choose somebody who knows you well from your family and personal life and somebody else who knows you well from your work life. The aim is to get a broad perspective on how you come across and to identify any blind spots. If you feel like taking yourself out of your comfort zone, it can be particularly valuable to choose at least one respondent who you don't always get along with.

QUICK 360 SURVEY

Thank you for agreeing to respond to the questions in this survey, the aim of which is to help me increase my self-awareness.

- What do you think are my 2-3 greatest strengths?
- What are the 1-3 areas where you think I could develop?
- What is the one thing you would change about me if you could?
- What else would you like me to know about myself?

MIRROR MOMENT: *Taking Your Own Advice*

When you reflect on yourself and your experience of everything in your life, in this moment, what is the best advice you need to hear and act on?

SELF-REGULATION

"A diamond is a piece of charcoal that handled stress exceptionally well."

\-

Anon

Self-regulation means having the ability to respond, as opposed to react to life. We all have an inner reaction to the things we see and hear around us but that doesn't mean we have to act on it. If we're self-regulating, it means we're able to override our default reaction and to instead choose our response for the best outcome.

Self-regulation is about being able to control or redirect disruptive moods and having the tendency to suspend judgement and to think before acting. It is the component of EQ that frees us from being prisoners or victims of our own emotions. Without self-regulation, self-awareness has no impact.

People who are self-regulating are aware of their inner conversation. They feel moods and emotional impulses just like everyone else, but they are able to control them and to channel their emotions in more useful ways. Self-regulation is what enables us to prevent emotional hijacking and access the logical part of our brain, allowing for innovative ways to overcome challenges.

Here's a simple and effective self-regulation technique that you can use to prevent your emotions from hijacking you, as well as your ability to think and behave the way you *want* to in any given situation.

TRAFFIC LIGHTS TECHNIQUE

STOP!
As soon as you see red, instead of reacting, think traffic lights and STOP!

WAIT!
Think about what you're about to say or do, think about them, take time to gain clarity

GO!
Choose your response instead of reacting

The hallmarks of self-regulation are the tendency for reflection and thoughtfulness; being comfortable with ambiguity and change; having integrity and the ability to resist impulsive urges. This doesn't only bring personal benefits but is an essential part of healthy relationships.

REALISATION PRACTICE: *Change Your Mind*

Choose from the following three levels to practice – be realistic about what is achievable for you and also try to stretch yourself over time.

Beginners: This takes 15 minutes and requires good self-regulation to stick with it…

Every minute pick a thought that produces positive feelings and hold onto the thought (and positive feelings) for 30 seconds. Then take 30 seconds to think of a new thought and hold onto it for a further 30 seconds and so on, until you have had 15 thoughts (it doesn't really matter if you choose the same thought but try to make them different). Really immerse yourself in the thought and associated feelings – turn up the volume and try to make the feelings intense.

Intermediate 1: This takes 30 minutes. Every minute, pick a thought that produces positive feelings and hold onto the thought (and positive feelings) for 50 seconds. Then take 10 seconds to think of a new thought and hold onto it for a further 50 seconds until you have had 30 thoughts (again, it doesn't really matter if you choose the same thought but try to make them different).

Intermediate 2: This takes 1 hour. Every minute, pick a thought that produces positive feelings and hold onto the thought (and the positive feelings) for 50 seconds. Then take 10 seconds to think of a new thought and hold onto it for a further 50 seconds until you have had 60 DIFFERENT thoughts.

Advanced: This takes 2 hours. Every minute, pick a thought that produces a positive feeling and hold onto the thought for 50 seconds. Then take 10 seconds to think of a new thought and hold onto it for a further 50 seconds until you have had 120 DIFFERENT thoughts.

MIRROR MOMENT: *Change Your Feelings*

It's easier to change your mind than it is to change your feelings, but it can still be done with a little practice.

Think of a person or situation that really frustrates you. Focus on the person or situation and what exactly frustrates or irritates you. Make it as real as possible! When you are fully conscious of how you are feeling, ask yourself the following questions…

How does this feeling serve me or the situation?
Am I willing to change how I feel? If not, why not?
How would I or the situation benefit if I change how I feel?
What needs to happen for me to consciously shift how I feel?

RELATIONSHIP AWARENESS

> "Empathy is about finding echoes
> of another person in yourself."
> -
> *Mohsin Hamid*

There's a wealth of evidence to support the claim that having good relationships and positive connections with others is the single most important predictor of good health, longevity and personal happiness. A number of experiments depriving babies of human contact have shown the devastating impact of a chronic lack of human connection and love at an early age. In 1989 Romanian dictator Nicolae Ceauşescu was overthrown and the world discovered that 170,000 children were being raised in orphanages. A team of three American psychologists saw a unique opportunity to study the effects of early institutionalisation. They began by assessing 136 children who had been living in Bucharest's institutions from birth and aged from 6 to 36 months. Then they randomly assigned half of the children to move into foster homes, while the other half remained in care. They also evaluated a control group of local children who had never lived in an institution. They found that the institutionalised children had delays in cognitive function, motor development and language. They showed deficits in socio-emotional behaviours and experienced more psychiatric disorders. They also showed changes in the patterns of electrical activity in their brains.

The need for human connection and love appears to be innate, but the ability to form healthy, loving relationships is learned. The fact is, somewhere within the depths of our heart we already know this. That is why we long for relationships that are meaningful and why these relationships can bring us such immense pleasure, and such immense pain... because they matter on a very deep and primal level.

Love is one of the most profound emotions known to human beings and is at the basis of most of our relationships: as parents, as children, as lovers, as friends. Of course, not all relationships require love to function; we have working relationships, customer relations, acquaintances at the gym, a next-door neighbour, a 'friend with benefits'... It's not about having all these relationships in place, it could be that you don't know your parents, you don't have children and you're perfectly happy being single. What matters is how happy you are with the relationships you do have. To raise our relationship awareness, we should be asking ourselves the following questions on a regular basis...

- How happy am I with the quality of my relationships?
- How would I like them to be different?
- What am I willing to do to achieve the relationships I want?

Most people have to work consciously to master the skills necessary to make relationships flourish. In order to master these skills, we need to first become self-aware, understand who we are and how to self-regulate our emotions and behaviours. We need to be aware of the impact we have on people and how to truly understand others.

Relationship Awareness means having an understanding and acceptance of the fact that other people do not necessarily see or feel things in the same way as we do. This is also know as empathy.

Empathy is described as the quality or process of entering fully, in our imagination, into another's feelings or motives. In the fullest sense, empathy implies putting yourself into the other person's shoes so that you really understand and appreciate their concerns, fears or more hopefully, their joy or enthusiasm. It also involves demonstrating this understanding. For example, arrogance is better understood by recognising that arrogant behaviour can often be driven by insecurity, lack of knowledge, or fear of looking stupid, or not belonging, or wanting to impress or to be valued.

You don't have to agree with another person to empathise with them. Often, when people say they can't *empathise* with this or that, what they really mean is that they can't *agree* with it.

Empathy is... having an understanding and appreciation of another person's feelings and point of view and showing that you understand.

Empathy is important because as a result of empathy we are able to establish rapport. Rapport is the quality of a close and harmonious relationship, in which the people or groups concerned really understand each others' feelings or ideas and communicate this well.

"Have you ever noticed that
anybody driving slower than you is an idiot,
and anyone going faster than you is a maniac?"

-

George Carlin

In the absence of empathy, we believe that we are proceeding at the 'perfect' speed and remain oblivious of the fact that we look like a 'maniac' or indeed an 'idiot' in the eyes of others!

Do you ever feel like you're surrounded by maniacs and idiots? Do you ever feel like you're surrounded by adults who behave like children? Or perhaps you feel like an eternal child who just hopes they don't get found out pretending to be a grown up? Have you found yourself being overprotective, over critical, or rebelling against a perfectly reasonable request? What all of these situations have in common is that you can understand them, notice them coming and manage them effectively, when you understand a simple model called Transactional Analysis, or TA.

Transactional Analysis, a social psychology theory originally developed by Dr. Eric Berne in the 1950s, can be used to improve our understanding of why we behave the way we do in certain relationships. The main idea is that we have three ego states: Parent, Adult and Child. All human behaviour and communication emerge from one of these three ego states and we can see this illustrated in the PAC model. Whoever we are relating to, whenever we communicate with each other, we do so from the position or ego state of a parent, adult or child. We encompass all three, but address others from one ego state at a time, depending on the relationship, how we are feeling and how the other person is behaving.

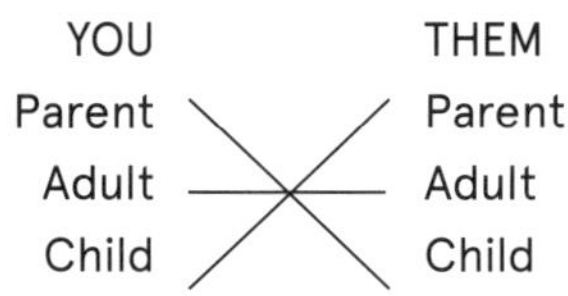

Parent Ego State

Parents, as defined in the PAC Model, are both emotional and reactive. They are worldly and experienced and therefore, speak critically of anything that doesn't match their perception of what's right and wrong – *their map of the world.* Obviously, Parents are caring too and aim to nurture and protect us.

Adult Ego State

Adults, as defined in the PAC Model, have their emotions in check and they consciously respond. They are agile and adaptable. They behave rationally, looking for the best outcome and trying to find the most effective way to achieve it. They have good emotional intelligence. They are self-aware and relate consciously.

Child Ego State

Children, as defined in the PAC Model, are also both emotional and reactive, sometimes it's difficult to distinguish between a

Child response and a *Parent* response. Children can do what they want and rebel against any kind of authority and they can also conform, be compliant and do as they are told.

In any conversation, *adult-to-adult* transactions are nearly always the ideal, with everyone responding consciously, speaking respectfully, looking for the best way forward and working together. However, if we are irritated or annoyed by something or someone, it's easy to slip into being a critical *Parent*. This only provokes the other person to respond as a *Child*. If we slip into the *Child* ego state ourselves and become rebellious or sarcastic towards them, this only brings out more of the critical Parent in them or prompts them to react as a Child and be rebellious back. These interactions don't tend to end well for anyone! So the next time you find yourself in any type of conflict, use the Traffic Lights technique that we introduced you to in Self-regulation, to stop yourself from reacting. Use the PAC model to become aware of the role or ego state that each of you is playing and ask yourself: *What would an Adult say?*

REALISATION PRACTICE: *Symptom vs Source*

STEP 1: Take a sheet of paper and divide it vertically into two halves. Write 'Symptom' at the top of the left-hand column and 'Source' at the top of the right-hand column. In the left-hand column only, make a list of behaviours that wind you up or that you find difficult to empathise with.

STEP 2: Think about what might be the underlying cause or source of each of the behaviours in your list. Write your ideas for the possible source of each of the behaviours in the right-hand column. For example, rudeness could be driven by fear, insecurity, lack of knowledge, personal issues or pain. If you find that the only answers you can come up with are still difficult to empa*thise with…* well, they're just like that or they enjoy doing that… recognise that this is a possibility. However, for the purposes of this exercise, which is about growing our ability to empathise, try to go beyond that and look for alternatives. The truth is that most people's bad behaviour is not intentional and there's often an understandable reason behind it. And remember, you definitely do not have to agree with or condone another person's thoughts, feelings or behaviour, in order to be able to understand and empathise with them.

STEP 3: Read the list in the left-hand column only and notice how you feel. Now read the list in the right-hand column and reflect on what's different about how you feel.

MIRROR MOMENT: *Seeking to Understand*

As we've already mentioned, empathy is the ability to understand and accept a different point of view or opinion. It does not mean agreeing with or condoning it. To what extent can you empathise with everything and everybody in your life, including yourself? Identify who or what it is that you cannot empathise with and reflect on what stops you.

RELATIONSHIP SKILLS

> "No one cares how much you know,
> until they know how much you care."
> -
> *Theodore Roosevelt*

Being skilled at relationships is in many ways the culmination of all the other dimensions of emotional intelligence. People tend to be very good at building and maintaining relationships when they can understand and regulate their own emotions and empathise with the feelings and perspectives of others, even when they strongly disagree with them.

When we have relationship skills, we are both authentic and able to speak to the authenticity in others. We do not seek to receive but to give. We nurture strong relationships naturally through love and communication. People who have strong relationship skills are trusting and generous, while maintaining healthy boundaries. They accept the differences and challenges that inevitably emerge. In fact, they are grateful for the insights gained from these moments. They enjoy their relationships… they love them.

The ability to form healthy relationships is learned. As a component of emotional intelligence, relationship skills means being good at forming and managing relationships and being able to create rapport and deal with conflict effectively. Being skilful at romantic relationships conjures up different things for different people. Usually, they have a few things in common; they openly give and receive affection and engage in honest dialogue about aspirations, values, needs and wants, including sex.

Good communication is integral to relationship skills, so it's important to understand how effective communication can be developed. A good conversation starts with the right mindset and intention. There's no trick and it's very simple; be present, stay curious and really listen to others and you will naturally build rapport and connection in any kind of conversation.

Researchers at Harvard found that seeking to establish a *common interest* as opposed to a position, is a key factor in productive conversations. One idea is to start by stating your interests (not your position) and asking for theirs. The more we can relate to someone, the more their defence mechanisms drop and we are able to avoid reactions like: *you're not listening, you don't understand me, you missed the point.* Relating is actually a cycle and each of the five steps that make up this cycle, are necessary for the creation of trust and rapport and as a result, better relationships.

THE RELATING CYCLE

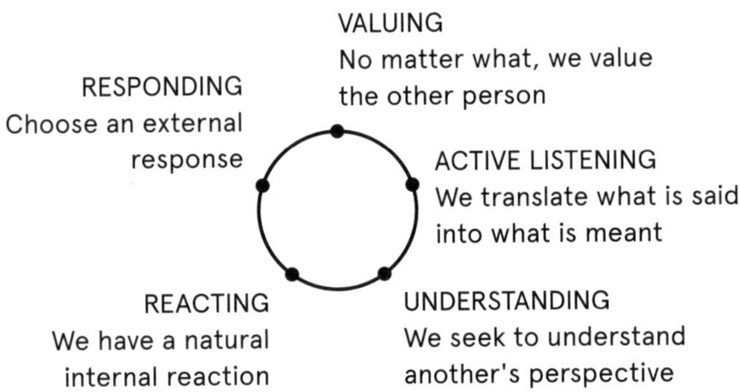

STEP 1: Valuing

Valuing another person assigns worth and importance to them and must be present at the start of the process. It is the foundation of good relationships. It is a choice to place the other person or people in high regard and give them significance. Valuing is done whether or not you believe they are worthy and regardless of personal opinion. Making this choice from the very start sets the tone of the relationship.

STEP 2: Active Listening

Listening goes beyond the obvious auditory hearing and even beyond the use of listening skills. Active Listening is about translating what is said into what is meant. Without the prior choice and commitment to value a person, you cannot hear them. Prejudices, preconceptions, attitudes, beliefs and values can interfere with active listening – it's like static on the line that inhibits clear transmission. In order to actively listen to another person, you need to be fully present. That means putting everything else, all distractions, all thoughts, all perceptions and planned responses, out of the moment.

STEP 3: Understanding

Understanding another person is choosing to give importance to what you hear them say and seeking to understand what they really mean. In the relating cycle, true understanding can only happen if we first place value on others by being present, in order to hear beyond the words. Understanding is not necessarily accepting what they say as your own perspective. It simply means you have understood that it's theirs. You may or may not identify with their perspective but you seek to understand it. Understanding is another internal process in the relating cycle. The other person may not see or perceive this but they will perceive your understanding – or lack of it – through your responses.

STEP 4: Reacting

We are all human and we all have an inner reaction to what we see and hear. It's spontaneous and natural. It cannot be avoided but it can be overcome. This is the only step in the relating cycle that isn't a choice and the way to overcome it is to notice it, accept it as a part of being human and to then make a conscious choice how to respond.

STEP 5: Responding

The final step in the cycle is to consciously choose our response. The quality of our response is what dictates the ability of others to relate to us. Being in control of our emotions and being able to avoid reacting and to instead respond in a way that is measured and appropriate, is the hallmark of *adult* communication and of advanced relationship skills.

Now here's a practice that will help you to stay adult in any kind of conversation, however challenging.

REALISATION PRACTICE: *3Fs*

3Fs is effective for having adult-to-adult communication, which we covered in Relationship Awareness.

F	>	Facts – State facts
F	>	Feelings – Show empathy
F	>	Further Actions – Next steps

An adult focuses on the *Facts* – separates fact from fiction and sticks to the facts. In relation to *Feelings* – an adult listens to concerns, shows empathy and uses 'I' and 'we' statements appropriately. When it comes to *Further Actions*, adults are solution orientated and focus on what can be done in terms of next steps.

When used in conjunction with the PAC model, the 3Fs can be really helpful for avoiding and resolving conflict, being assertive, and for having the kind of uncomfortable conversations that the child in us would much rather avoid!

You can use the three simple steps that follow as guidelines when you put your new insights into practice…

STEP 1: Before the conversation

Identify the person in your life that you find the most difficult to relate to and apply your awareness of PAC and the 3Fs. Think about the last difficult conversation you had with them, which of the three ego states were you in? Now reflect and make a note of how your *adult* side would deal with the situation if you had your chance again.

STEP 2: During the conversation

The next time you find yourself in a conversation that's in danger of getting difficult and turning into conflict, use the Traffic Light technique to stop yourself reacting; use the PAC model to recognise which ego state you and the other person are in. Then use the 3Fs to stick to the *facts,* empathise with their *feelings* first before sharing your own and to have a discussion about *further actions* and the way forward that will benefit you both.

To help you stay on track, follow this How to Be an Adult Checklist:

1. *Acknowledge their point of view first* – as Steven Covey famously said, seek first to understand and then to be understood. Listen and empathise even if you disagree with what you hear. Genuinely seek to understand and let them know what you have understood. It may take a while for you to see their viewpoint clearly. Remember not to jump in with your own point of view yet... you will get your turn soon.
2. *Separate fact from fiction* – look at the facts openly without assumption, exaggeration or distortion. Remember that the way someone else feels is a fact. If that's how they feel, then it's a fact!
3. *Share your point of view* – without trying to prove a point, attacking, blaming or belittling theirs.
4. *Co-create a solution that respects each other* – show a genuine willingness to work together on a solution that respects and takes into account both points of view.

STEP 3: after the conversation

Reflect and respond to the following questions:

- What percentage of time were you being an *adult*?
- What impact did being an *adult* have?
- What impact did not being an *adult* have?
- What would you do differently next time?

MIRROR MOMENT: *Back To The Future*

Now, a look into the future! First read the four questions below. Make sure you won't be disturbed for five minutes, make yourself comfortable, close your eyes, and imagine you're having a conversation with yourself… when you're 80.

Which relationships really mattered in my life? Which relationships did not?

- How happy am I with the way I loved others in my life?
- Which relationships deserved more of my time and energy?
- Which relationships did not?
- What advice can you give me so I can have better relationships?

SELF-ASSESSMENT

- When it comes to my emotional well-being, where am I doing well?
- Where is there room for improvement?
- What do I want to work on?
- Where do I want to focus primarily?
- On a scale of 1-10 (10 is high) how satisfied am I with the level of my current, overall emotional well-being?

SELF-COACHING: *What would love do?*

You will probably have identified one or more areas where you can improve your emotional well-being. Choose which of these you want to start with and write a short opening statement that best describes it as the topic you want to focus on. E.g. *I find it really difficult to keep my cool when my students misbehave in class and I avoid confronting them by pretending it's not happening. I know that's not a solution, but I don't know what else to do. You can then repeat this process for each of the areas you want to work on.*

STEP 1: What would love ask?

Imagine it's a loved one and not yourself that you're talking to and that it's *their* topic. If the aim of this step is to know what the 'other person' wants, what question/s do you want to ask in order to understand? And how would you answer each of those question/s?

STEP 2: What would love say?

Imagine it's a loved one and not yourself that you're talking to and it's *their* answer/s, what would you say in response and how would you say it?

STEP 3: What would love do?

Imagine it's a loved one and not yourself that you're talking to and it's *their* topic you are offering advice on, what would you advise them to do?

STEP 4: What stops you?

Based on this inner dialogue, what stops you from taking your own advice and acting from a place of self-love? If nothing is stopping you, then all you need to do is take action. If something is stopping you, go back to STEP 1 and repeat the cycle – but focus on your answer to this question – until you know what to do, how and when to do it, and there's nothing else stopping you.

SPIRITUAL

"Behaving with wisdom and compassion,
while maintaining inner and outer peace,
regardless of the situation."

-

C. Wigglesworth

The way we define spiritual intelligence or SQ, is through four main elements: *Higher Self-awareness, Self-mastery, Universal Awareness* and *Universal Mastery.*

HIGHER SELF-AWARENESS – distinguishing between our ego reactions and our inner wisdom
SELF-MASTERY – shifting from ego to higher self, acting on our inner wisdom, self-love
UNIVERSAL AWARENESS – awareness of the interconnectedness of all things
UNIVERSAL MASTERY – sovereignty, agency, free will, universal love

Spiritual intelligence is still a new and perhaps radical idea for some, but so was emotional intelligence a few decades ago and now it's common knowledge. Before we explore the topic of spiritual intelligence, it's important first to be clear what we mean by 'spiritual' and to separate spirituality from any kind of dogma, set of practices, or religion. For us, spirituality and metaphysics are synonymous and describe those aspects of our reality that are unseen or 'meta' (beyond) physical. The spiritual aspect or realm of being human covers our innate need to belong and connect to something larger than ourselves and to find greater meaning in our lives. Spiritual *intelligence* has a more specific meaning and is about being able to distinguish between our ego (acting from fear) and our true or *higher self* (acting from love), to then consciously choose the perspective of our higher self as the lens through which we experience and express ourselves in life.

When you make the shift from ego to higher self, it doesn't mean the ego dissolves and you metamorphosize into a saintly being beyond reproach. Your ego is still there, it's just not in charge anymore because you've identified another aspect of yourself that was always there and that knows better. You've realised that you are an integral part of the innate wisdom that some have described as 'deep intelligence' and so is everyone else, without exception. It is the acknowledgment of self as an integral part of the whole, including whatever creative force you believe created all this and it gives you full access to all areas. For example, it becomes clear that everything is connected to everything on all levels. From this perspective, the notion that we are all one is a distinct possibility, if not a certainty. Paradoxically, this makes authenticity paramount and any attempt to be someone other than yourself makes no sense. Suddenly, being you to the best of your ability is the most important job in the world.

Our differences and everything we are as individuals are evidence of our unity not of our separateness. What makes you unique is all the things that make you different and distinct – but not *separate* – from everyone else. We need to get into the practice of celebrating our differences and valuing our uniqueness because these are the gifts that we each bring as our contribution to the whole.

The shift from ego to higher self is not always an easy one. Some describe it as an 'emptying out', that can take us on a bumpy ride through the full spectrum of difficult feelings and emotions… discomfort, hopelessness, emptiness, despondency, even desolation… before the process brings joy, passion, synchronicity, abundance, well-being, fulfilment and *love*, back into our life.

"The more heart-centred support
and authentic encouragement you offer yourself
as emptying out occurs, whether you feel
the love or not, invites you through the doorway
of unity consciousness to discover
a new frontier of reality."

-

Matt Kahn

So spiritual intelligence is about the esoteric journey from ego to higher self, that enables us to transcend polarity consciousness and the belief that we are all separate competing with each other for scarce resources; to shift into unity consciousness and unconditional love for everything and everyone, including ourselves. The result is a far greater sense of our birth right of personal *sovereignty* and of *agency* as the author of our own life. Ultimately, it's about being conscious of our *free will* to be here and live life as our authentic self.

HIGHER SELF-AWARENESS

"Every man is a divinity in disguise,
a god playing the fool."

-

Ralph Waldo Emerson

The process of developing a greater awareness of both ego and higher self is not necessarily quick or easy, but it's empowering. It prepares us for self-mastery, which is the shift from ego to higher self.

Through the ages, the higher self has had many names: the inner self, soul, Christ-consciousness, Buddha-nature, Spirit and authentic self. Yet despite all the descriptions and definitions, many of us still struggle to understand the higher self and its role in our lives. So how do we transform this important subject from an intellectual concept into something that we experience to live a better life?

First, we need to accept that the path is not direct and we need to get to know our ego a little better, before attempting such an undertaking as connecting with our higher self. No matter how much work we've done or how spiritually aware we become, we all have a 'lower self' or ego, as a lifelong companion. Contrary to what many people think, the aim is not to get rid of ego, it's for the ego to be in the passenger seat and the higher self behind the wheel.

So, let's take a closer look at the different aspects of ego:

- I am what I have (possessions)
- I am what I do (achievements)
- I am what others think of me (reputation)
- I am separate from everyone and everything (I am only physical)
- I am lacking this or that

The higher self knows that none of this is true. This is just the content of our lives and yet most of us think it's this that defines us. It's how we present ourselves; by name, where we live, education, work, relationship status. But that's not who we are, it's who the ego thinks we are. So, when you become aware of your ego, it doesn't mean that you know who you are, it means that *you know who you are not*. The more limited and narrow our view of ourselves, the more we react to the limitations of the ego and the unconscious words and actions of others. The faults we perceive in them become their identity in our eyes and our ego loves it because it makes us feel better about ourselves. Instead of looking beyond the ego in others to the divinity that is in us all, we look at the ego. The moment we realise that what we react to in others is also in us, is the moment we become aware of our own ego. We also realise what we are doing to others is what we thought others were doing to us and we stop seeing ourselves as hapless victims.

Becoming more conscious of our higher self involves a state of knowingness that breaks away from ego, leaving behind old belief systems, attitudes and distortions of the truth that no longer serve us. It feels like taking off the blinkers that have for so long limited our perception and experience of life… and it changes everything!

When we develop *self-mastery*, we not only listen to our higher self but start to embody or *be* it. Our positive emotions let us know when we are aligned with our higher self and our negative feelings let us know when we are not. In that sense, they act as an *emotional barometer*. You can grow your awareness of the state you are operating from in any given moment, by recognising your feelings as indicators.

Lower Self (Ego): Fear, anxiety, depression, revenge, hatred, jealousy, possessiveness, righteousness, anger.

Higher Self: Wisdom, unconditional love, compassion, forgiveness, happiness, bliss, gratitude, purpose, intuition, inspiration, humility.

Another way of growing your awareness of your higher self is to start listening to your *intuition*… your '*in-tuition*'… the 'quieter voice' within your inner dialogue. Your higher self doesn't need to shout like your ego – it has nothing to prove! Therefore, it can be easy to miss your 'higher voice'. You will have experienced this from time-to-time: *"I knew I shouldn't have done that"* or *"I wish I'd listened to myself"*. We're not suggesting that you follow through with every quiet thought that you have, but do listen and pay attention, use your *emotional barometer* to discern what best serves you or the situation.

When making important decisions, we humans do appear to have something of a bias towards rational thought and will often ignore the inner voice – if it doesn't match what our logic tells us. But we've noticed over the years that all the successful people we meet, definitely listen to their inner guidance. In fact, we have yet to meet or hear of a successful entrepreneur or great leader who doesn't but not in isolation. As with most things, it's all about balance and our best decisions are the result of intuition and rational thinking.

Intuitive people are good at listening to their bodies and talk about having 'gut feelings'. Recent advances in brain science mean we now know why and it's because we have an extraordinary number of high-performing brain cells in our digestive system that are clearly overqualified for just waste-disposal duty! It's called the *enteric nervous system* and sometimes the 'second brain' and it can operate independently of the brain in our skull and of the central nervous system. We're still learning about how it all works and what it all means but the more we learn, the more we understand just how important it is to relate to ourselves more holistically and to listen to what our spirit, our heart, our mind and our body are telling us.

Some of us find listening to our intuition comes easily and for others it takes a little practice, but we all have it. Introverts are often more intuitive because they spend more time alone… even when there are other people in the room. But whether or not it comes naturally to you, spending more time in solitude is a good way of becoming more intuitive. Meditation and other mindfulness practices are also great ways of tuning in to your inner guidance. They help quiet the mind and they are also key to the growth of self-knowledge. Research published in the journal, *Perspectives on Psychological Science,* defined mindfulness as 'paying attention to one's current experience in a non-judgmental way' and simply put, there are few things you can do that are more effective for gaining a better understanding of your own personality.

Also pay attention to *synchronicity.* Synchronicities are events that are clearly connected but not by the usual logic of cause-and-effect. Synchronicity is evidence of what in classical times were called '*sympathies*' – a rather beautiful and poetic way of describing the interconnectedness of internal and external – the dance between mind and matter. Carl Jung believed that synchronicities mirror deep psychological processes and carry meaning and guidance in the same way as our dreams. For example, you might be trying to decide whether or not to accept a job offer and you pass a billboard with a Nike ad that says, Just Do It! It's just an ad and it's directed at millions of people but in that moment, in the context of your life, it feels like a direct message that is specific to you.

Not every *coincidence* is a synchronicity. You can derive meaning when an external event *coincides* with an event on the inside. If you've just seen an article about being pregnant and then you notice two pregnant women taking a stroll, it doesn't mean the universe is trying to send you a message related to starting a family. But it might if there was something internal going on for you related to pregnancy at that particular time. As a rule of thumb, if it means something to you, then a coincidence becomes a synchronicity. In *The Way of the Shaman,* anthropologist Michael Harner, describes synchronicity as 'a kind of homing beacon analogous to a radio directional signal indicating that the right procedures and methods are being employed.'

You can call it confirmation bias if you want to, but for us, synchronicities are nothing less than little miracles that are happening all the time and only some of which we notice. No one has been able to fully explain them, but perhaps we should simply accept them as little glimpses of the universe and evidence of much more than meets the eye. Synchronicities are not as rare as you think and the more of them you notice, the more of them you have.

To test this theory, begin recording them when they happen. Easily done, use your phone or keep a notebook handy to jot them down as they occur. Be discerning and be aware that we all need to learn to recognise the difference between what is and what isn't true.

REALISATION PRACTICE: *Being You on Purpose*

In this practice you are going to pick a time when you will consciously and purposefully be You, which means the real You, the big You, the one with the capital 'Y'… otherwise known as your higher self.

To achieve this will require that you draw on all the insights that you've gained so far from working with this book and most noticeably, how to listen to your inner dialogue, identify the voice that comes from your higher self and act on it.

Begin by reflecting on how good you are at identifying and acting from your higher self as opposed to your ego. How good are you at responding as opposed to reacting to the world around you? How self-regulating are you? If you believe you're already pretty good at being your higher self in everyday life, then choose the more challenging option of being your higher self for a whole week. If you are less confident, then lower your expectations accordingly. What is important, is to set yourself up for success from the start and work your way up until you are confident and comfortable being *You.*

Choose the level at which you would like to start the practice from the below options and unless you go in at the top end, work your way up at your own pace, until you have been successful at each level:

Level 1: Identify one event in your diary for the day and commit to yourself that you will listen to your higher self and act on it, as opposed to your ego. In other words, during that event (a PTA meeting at your son's school, drinks with a friend, visiting your mother, going to the supermarket, a phone call to your bank), you commit to consciously focus on your inner dialogue, identify the inner thoughts and responses that are coming from your higher self and act on those.

Level 2: Choose one morning, afternoon or evening (a four-hour period) this week and commit to yourself that you will listen to your higher self and act on it, as opposed to your ego. Consciously focus on your inner dialogue, identify the inner thoughts and responses that are coming from your higher self and act on those.

Level 3: Choose one day this week and commit to yourself that you will listen to your higher self and act on it, as opposed to your ego. In other words, from the time you wake up to the time you go to sleep, you will consciously focus on your inner dialogue, identify the inner thoughts and responses that are coming from your higher self and act on those.

Level 4: For one whole week, commit to yourself that you will listen to your higher self and act on it, as opposed to your ego. In other words, from the time you wake up to the time you go to sleep, you will consciously focus on your inner dialogue, identify the inner thoughts and responses that are coming from your higher self and act on those.

Level 5: What, if anything, is stopping you from listening to your higher self and acting on it all the time?

Each time you complete a level, reflect on the impact. Was anything different or unusual? What did you notice about yourself? What did you notice about others? What did you think? How did you feel? How did you behave?

MIRROR MOMENT: *Being Your Higher Self*

Reflect on a challenging situation that you have in your life right now, notice any negative thoughts or feelings you engage in like anger, doubt, fear, worry, discouragement, resentment, etc. Then ask yourself this question; how does my higher self see this and how does that change how I think and feel about it?

SELF-MASTERY

"I have decided to be happy
because it is good for my health."
-
Voltaire

Self-mastery is a path, a commitment to never-ending improvement; it's a process of becoming and transcending. Becoming the best version of ourselves, while transcending the worst version. It's not about controlling yourself or eliminating those conflicting, fearful, aggressive, defensive, jealous, depressive and other egoic aspects of ourselves. It's about getting to know these parts and then transcending them. It's an internal knowing that you are evolving into higher aspects of yourself. It's from here that you can truly master the gifts and talents that you have.

Self-mastery means preventing our ego from taking over while seeking guidance and taking action from our higher self. Shifting from conditioned egoic responses to the wisdom and loved-based responses of the higher self, while creating the reality that we want. When you manifest from your higher self, it becomes less about *'asking and receiving'* and more about being in a constant state of *'open to receiving'*. We allow our higher self to be in the driving seat. So higher self-awareness is essential but just being aware of our higher self is not enough. Self-mastery is about *being* and *acting* on this awareness. We realise who and what we really are, actualising our potential in the process. We take full responsibility and accountability for our life… for better and for worse.

It's often when things get worse rather than better that we get the chance to find out who's driving – our ego or our higher self? The phone rings and you find out that someone has dented your car; your holiday company has gone bust, your child didn't get that school place, your shares just nosedived, there are no toilet rolls on the shelves because of panic buying and hoarding by others. If it's your ego driving, there's an emotional hijacking that tells you there's something much more important to you than the peace and love and happiness that was all you needed a moment ago. You certainly don't feel either responsible or accountable. So how do you feel at that moment? What goes on in your inner dialogue? It may not be what you want to feel or what you want to hear, but this ongoing self-observation is 'the work' that leads to self-knowledge and ultimately answers the question, *who am I?*

"I am the master of my fate
and the captain of my destiny."

-

Nelson Mandela

The key to mastery in anything, is practice. But at this stage of the game, if we have high PQ, IQ, EQ and an awareness of our higher self, we are primed to be the best we can be and enjoy the process of becoming; we feel in 'flow' and we gratefully ride the rollercoaster of life. We are self-motivating, self-actualising and self-loving… unconditionally! We are values-based and purpose-driven and we trust that no matter what life throws us, we can handle it. We accept what is, we are comfortable with the unknown and we know when to allow things to unfold in their own time. We have a fundamental belief that *the Universe has got our back.*

"Imagine what it will be like to have no boundaries or limitations, to be free, and for all your actions to be spontaneously correct and all desires spontaneously fulfilled. Imagine self-mastery, it's here waiting for you right now."

-

Deepak Chopra

Self-mastery is synonymous with authenticity. Be *yourself*, because that's who you really are. Live from this place and you will create ever more experiences that serve you and others too. Usually, when a person gains a level of self-mastery, they begin to inspire and help others. In fact, this is one of the many natural by-products of self-mastery.

Of course, there will be times when our higher-self 'speaks' and we choose to ignore it. Whether or not we later regret that decision, what is important is that we're aware of and take full responsibility for that choice. This is all part of attaining self-mastery. Maintaining positive momentum is essential and will help you reconnect more fully with your higher self. Fill every day with gratitude. As you go through your day, regularly express your gratitude for everything you can think of. Forgive yourself and others and let go of the past. Realise that there is no need to 'forgive and forget', you can still acknowledge that you or somebody else has done something wrong, while at the same time forgiving. Non-forgiveness feels dense and heavy because it binds you energetically to the other person and your lower self/ego.

Those on the spiritual path already know the importance and power of *forgiveness*. Forgiving something is not the same as agreeing with or condoning it. Rather it is a critical and powerful choice by the person who has been 'wronged', that enables them to stay in full control and hold the reins of their own healing, independent of the perspective and actions of the person that wronged them.

In our approach, *acceptance* is a higher form of forgiveness and both are expressions of genuine love. Like forgiveness, at its heart, acceptance is about transcending our instinctive response to hurt them back or retaliate. This letting go when healthy, stems from a caring understanding that it's in the highest interest of the wronged person's life to do so. Like compassion, both acceptance and forgiveness invite all parties to see and understand self and others empathically, as human beings, in the context of natural life processes that albeit painful, are ultimately designed for their highest good. It takes an enormous amount of courage to not forgive prematurely, to allow the other to step in and make amends in order to repair a relationship. Forgiveness and acceptance are essential ingredients of learning to live and love *wholeheartedly*. If you haven't seen Brene Brown's TED Talk about the *Power of Vulnerability* in which she presents the findings of her research and the qualities of wholeheartedness, then it's definitely worth a watch.

Whether you choose acceptance or fear in relation to a past betrayal, transgression or mistreatment, make no mistake that your response accordingly shapes both the present and future. It's a choice between allowing automatic defence strategies to decide the course of your life, or consciously accessing the strength of both your courage and your compassion by choosing acceptance. It's important to take time to consider this because your choices are powerful emotional energies, fuelled by your beliefs, wants, yearnings, thoughts and actions, etc., that powerfully determine the direction that your life takes.

Acceptance is a transformative emotional stance in life that, in addition to being energy efficient, is a form of unconditional love. It is infinitely more powerful than fear, shame or guilt, forcing one into forgiving too easily or prematurely. Or not forgiving at all.

When we have self-mastery, not only do we have forgiveness through acceptance, we also have a deeper sense of gratitude for everything, from the most mundane to our greatest challenges.

Before going to bed each night, write down five things that you are grateful for each day, for one week. They don't have to be big things. You can give thanks and appreciate the seemingly insignificant things in life; electricity, fresh water coming out of the tap, the post being delivered etc., the things we take for granted that support our existence but rarely get a second thought.

After a challenging event, it's more difficult to be grateful but gratitude isn't an emotion that's reserved for when you get what you want. When things go wrong you can use the power of gratitude to release some of the negative emotions that you may be feeling due to a failure or setback that you just experienced.

After a negative or unfortunate event, put things in perspective by remembering that every difficulty carries within it the seeds of an equal or greater benefit. When faced with adversity, ask yourself the following questions:

- What's good about this?
- What can I learn from this?
- How can I benefit from this?
- What is it about this that I can be grateful for?

REALISATION PRACTICE: *Self-Actualising*

In psychology, self-actualisation is achieved when you're able to reach your full potential. Being truly self-actualised is considered the exception rather than the rule, since most people are working to meet more pressing needs. It's about having a desire which is present in everyone, to develop your potential to the full.

This is not a destination. You don't actually ever reach the point of self-actualisation, which is why we say that. However much we learn about ourselves and develop, we are all *self-actualising* and none of us are *self-actualised.* It's a lifelong journey that represents motivation of the highest order, driving us to realise our true potential and become our 'best self.' To self-actualise, you must always strive to expand your horizons as a human being. Abraham Maslow studied the shared characteristics of individuals who are self-actualising.

What follows are excerpts from Maslow's work in which he describes the characteristics and features of self-actualising people. As you read through his descriptions, reflect on how you're doing as a self-actualising human being.

1. DISCERNMENT

"Self-actualizing people have an unusual ability to detect the spurious, the fake, and the dishonest in personality, and in general to judge people correctly and efficiently."

Maslow found that self-actualising people could spot inconsistencies or concealed realities far more easily than the average person, which could easily be mistaken for 'good taste or good judgment,' but which he concluded was based on consistency of perception.

2. ACCEPTANCE

"They can accept their own human nature, with all its shortcomings, with all its discrepancies from the ideal image without feeling real concern."

Self-actualising people lack overriding guilt, crippling shame, and extreme anxiety. They are more content with life and all of its shortcomings. The self-actualising person is also able to enjoy their 'animal-nature', without feelings of regret, shame or apology. This is not to say that they never experience guilt or shame, they just experience it in appropriate amounts and are rarely hindered by it.

3. SPONTANEITY

"Their behaviour is marked by simplicity and naturalness, and by lack of artificiality or straining for effect. His unconventionality is not superficial but essential or internal... and he is perhaps more human, more revealing of the original nature of the species."

They have a rich and unconventional inner world and have no problem fitting in when needing to adapt to social norms.

4. WORLD-CENTRIC

"Self-actualising people are in general, strongly focused on problems outside themselves... they are not generally much concerned about themselves... these individuals customarily have some mission in life, some task to fulfil, some problem outside themselves which enlists much of their energies."

Self-actualising people tend to live in the widest possible frame of reference and see the bigger picture. This ability to see the world like this has social and interpersonal importance. Creating peace, serenity and less stress for themselves.

5. DETACHMENT

"For all my subjects it is true that they can be solitary without harm to themselves and without discomfort… it is true for almost all that they positively like solitude and privacy to a definite greater degree than the average person."

According to Maslow, self-actualising people are often undisturbed by that which produces stress in others. This is one of the first things that people notice about self-actualising people; they have the ability to remain calm and serene through crises and misfortune and practice independent thinking and decision making.

6. AUTONOMY

"Self-actualising people are not dependent for their main satisfactions on the real world, or other people or culture or means to ends or, in general, on extrinsic satisfactions. Rather, they are dependent on their own development and continued growth of their own potentialities."

Independent of the opinion of others, their focus is on intrinsic rather than extrinsic rewards. This state of autonomy can sometimes be mistaken for rebellion, especially by those who seek to control others.

7. HUMAN KINSHIP

"Self-actualising people have for human beings in general, a deep feeling of identification, sympathy, and affection in spite of the occasional anger, impatience, or disgust... because of this they have a genuine desire to help the human race as if they were all members of a single family."

A genuine love for and desire to help all people is often tempered by sadness and disappointment in the self-imposed limitations of the average person. Their ability to empathise can often result in their taking on the role of the elder.

8. HUMILITY

"All my subjects may be said to be democratic people in the deepest possible sense... they can be and are friendly with anyone of a suitable character regardless of class, education, political belief, race or colour... it is as if they are not even aware of these differences."

All the guilt, anxiety and insecurity of being human, along with the belief that we can learn from anyone and that even the worst person has redeeming features.

9. APPRECIATION

"Self-actualising people have the wonderful capacity to appreciate again and again, freshly and naively, the basic goods of life with awe, pleasure, wonder and even ecstasy, however stale these experiences may have become to others... for such a person, any sunset may be as beautiful as the first one."

The self-actualising person has a beginner's mind, a childlike curiosity and the ability to see beauty in everything. This is a spirit of playfulness that never seems to dull with age. As Maslow put it; for the self-actualising person the thousandth flower is just as beautiful as the first.

10. ETHICS

"These individuals are strongly ethical, they have definite moral standards, they do right and do not do wrong. Needless to say, their notions of right and wrong and good and evil are often not the conventional ones."

Clear, albeit unconventional ideas of right and wrong. Self-actualising people rarely need to debate right and wrong because they have an innate and often an unorthodox sense of it.

11. HUMOUR

"They do not laugh at hostile humour or superiority humour... characteristically what they consider humour is more closely allied to philosophy than anything else... more akin to parables or fables."

Self-actualising people can laugh at themselves and see the divine comedy in humanity, with all its shortcomings. They do not make jokes or laugh at the expense of other individuals or groups of people.

12. CREATIVITY

"Each one shows in one way or another a special kind of creativeness or originality or inventiveness that has certain peculiar characteristics... which is akin to the universal creativeness of unspoiled children."

Maslow goes on to say that this creativity is different than that of a musician or an artist. It is more related to the self-actualizing person's ability to do anything they are engaged in with a certain style. It is as if they are less inhibited or don't care as much about how other people view them or their actions. This brings with their actions a certain freedom and beauty.

This creativity is also intricately linked to *spontaneity* and *appreciation*, which are themselves closely related to the childlike quality of finding joy in even the most mundane tasks.

13. OPTIMISM

"The science of psychology has been far more successful on the negative than on the positive side… It has revealed to us much about man's shortcomings, his illnesses, his sins, but little about his potentialities, his virtues, his achievable aspirations or his psychological health… We must find out what psychology might be if it could free itself from the stultifying effects of limited, pessimistic and stingy preoccupations with human nature."

Self-actualising people take a positive view of things and see the world as abundant and benevolent. Maslow wasn't talking about 'false' optimism or positive thinking as a technique, but about a worldview that sincerely expects good things to happen and accepts it when they do not.

14. CULTURAL TRANSCENDENCE

"Self-actualising people are not well adjusted (in the naive sense of approval of and identification with the culture). They get along with the culture in various ways, but of all of them it may be said that in a certain profound and meaningful sense, they resist encul-

turation and maintain inner detachment from the culture in which they are immersed."

Self-actualising people have the ability to see beyond the confines of culture and era and rarely identify with any organisation or culture. This means that they are able to transcend the collective mindset and social conditioning that is an inherent part of culture.

15. PEAK EXPERIENCES

"Peaking self-actualising people tend to live in a realm of being, of poetry, aesthetics, symbols, transcendence, 'religion' of the mystical, personal, non-institutional sort, and of end-experiences."

Self-actualising people tend to feel and experience life to the fullest extent, they have peak experiences involving intense enjoyment and feelings of bliss and that results in a sense of timelessness, loss of ego and intense presence.

Interestingly, Maslow found that the more his subjects recalled and talked about peak experiences, the more peak experiences they had.

MIRROR MOMENT: *This Is Your Life*

Whether or not you buy into the idea that we choose the life we are in, in order to learn something, take a moment to imagine it is true and ask yourself: Why did I choose this life?

UNIVERSAL AWARENESS

"We are here to awaken from the illusion
of our separateness."
-
Thich Nhat Hanh

The romantic and radical notion that we are all one, made of the same 'golden stardust', was popularised by the iconic rock star Joni Mitchell, back in the heady new age of the 60's and rubber-stamped as scientific fact more recently by Britain's favourite TV physicist, Brian Cox. It seems paradoxical to say authenticity is paramount when we are all an integral part of the whole, but what would be the point of the whole without its constituent parts? Our hypothesis is that we are each the unique expression and experience of consciousness co-creating reality. In other words, it is only because we are each unique as individuals that there exists a whole and the more we get to know ourselves from the inside out, the more conscious of this we become and the more aware of being not just part of the whole but of having the whole within us. From this perspective we start to truly celebrate authenticity in ourselves and others.

It is only when we have identified and truly accepted our authentic self, that we start to heal and open the door to appreciation and love of self. And that is what this book has been about – learning to know, appreciate and love who *I Am.* Just that. Without the need to be, do, have or achieve, anything more than that which *You Are.*

From this perspective of unity consciousness there is only You, infinite love and potential; the relationship with self is not just the most important relationship we ever have, it is the *only* relationship we ever have. Everyone and everything else we encounter is a reflection of this basic truth. As within, so without, as above, so below. Our growth happens horizontally and vertically. The more we work on *expressing* self through our physical, cognitive, emotional and spiritual aspects, the more scope we develop for *experiencing* self and this in turn broadens our spectrum of influence and impact. We expand in every direction.

This realisation of oneness – of the fact that everyone and everything is intrinsically linked – is the outcome of clarity and is what prepares us for *universal mastery.* It places us in a state of *unity consciousness* from where we make wise and compassionate choices and decisions that are beneficial to ourselves, to others and to the world.

Whenever we make wise and compassionate choices, it benefits us all. That includes people now and for generations to come, the planet and even the natural order or cosmos. Indigenous people from around the world have always known this and have always understood themselves as an integral part of nature and of the cosmos. We however, need to practice being with nature because most of us have become disconnected and perceive ourselves as separate from the natural world. Countless studies have shown that reconnecting to nature positively impacts our wellbeing, resilience, presence, concentration, immune system, as well as our sense of gratitude and love for life itself. Jon Young, a world leader in nature connection, has described one of the main benefits as, *"A deep ethic born of conscious awareness of our interdependence with all others resulting in a commitment to service to others, the future generations, conservation, sustainability and regenerative living principles"*.

One of the easiest and most natural ways of tapping into the power of nature is to find yourself a *sit-spot,* which simply means a place outdoors – garden, park, allotment, beach, forest, balcony – where you can spend time sitting in present awareness, observing the flow of reality as it occurs around you. The perfect sit-spot is the one that works best for you and you can find it by using the following three criteria:

- A place in nature you can get to regularly (preferably close by).
- A place you can go to in all weather, all seasons, and at different times of day.
- A place you can be *alone – all one* – with nature.

Visit your sit-spot regularly, every day if possible, for as long as you like but for at least 15 minutes at a time. Turn off or at least silence your mobile phone. Sit or stand as you prefer, do whatever it is that you do to bring yourself to a state of present awareness and observe with all your senses. Absorb whatever is happening around you; birds singing, leaves rustling, the warmth of the sun on your skin and become consciously aware of the fact that you're part of all this and that it's all part of something much bigger. If you do this regularly, you'll soon begin to feel the benefits to your sense of well-being of bringing nature back into your life, as well as feeling more deeply and fundamentally connected with every aspect of life.

REALISATION PRACTICE: *I Am That*

Here's an interesting exercise, inspired by the work of Ken Wilbur and the Integral movement that helps reduce polarity consciousness and increase unity consciousness, by reducing the illusion of polarity and bringing down the barriers between 'us and them'. This can take anything from a few minutes to over an hour. What's important is that the process results in the third-person 'it', becoming a first-person 'I'.

What this does is to integrate our 'shadows' (those parts of self we reject or deny) into our conscious awareness. When we stop wasting our energy 'boxing with our own shadow', we have more energy for living a better life.

STEP 1: Think of a person, a thing, an event or circumstance, that triggers an emotional reaction in you, either positive or negative. Write down on paper from a third-person perspective, a description of what it is that triggers you. The aim in this first step is to bring awareness and gain clarity on what appears to be the cause of your emotional reaction. Take time to write as much detail as possible in the third-person, in other words, as if you are an observer.

STEP 2: Now have a conversation in your head with them/it and write the dialogue down from both perspectives. Just make up how you imagine they/it would react or respond if you explained how you feel and what it is about them/it that makes you feel like that. Go into as much depth and detail as you feel necessary.

STEP 3: Finally, take the position of the person/thing/event/circumstance that triggered the reaction and write it down from purely their perspective. Here you embody whatever trait or behaviour you feel caused your emotional reaction, drawing from the insights gained during Step 2. E.g. *It's not just about them, it's about me too!* In other words, the second person process results in the first person *embodiment* of the characteristic or trait that was perceived as something in them/it, but not in you. If this doesn't happen it's difficult, if not impossible, to hold the position of first person. *If you cannot identify with it then you cannot embody it.*

This simple exercise illustrates how vital it is for us to be conscious of our language and that of others because... *language is never innocent!* Third person language objectifies something, putting it firmly outside of ourselves, making it about 'her', 'him', 'them', 'it'...

MIRROR MOMENT: *Polarity and Beyond*

Universal Awareness is that beautiful space where we know that we truly are connected to all things.

"You are not separate from the whole.
You are one with the sun, the earth, the air.
You don't have a life. You are life."

-

Eckhart Tolle

You can consciously connect to that space now. Get comfortable and become aware of your breathing. Breathe through your nose, slowly and consciously. Allow your thoughts to come and go without judgment. If your mind starts to wander, gently bring your focus back to your breathing.

Become conscious of the wave of energy of becoming one with Earth and the Universe; one with your own and all other bodies; one with the visible and the invisible.

Be still for a few minutes, savour your connection to all that is and without the need to have any answers, ponder or meditate on some of life's big questions:

- What is beyond birth and death?
- What is beyond duality?
- What is infinity?

UNIVERSAL MASTERY

"Our task must be to free ourselves from
this prison by widening our circle of compassion
to embrace all living creatures and the whole
of nature in its beauty."

-

Albert Einstein

The words cosmos and universe are interchangeable. Using the word *'cosmos'* in place of the word *'universe'* adds another layer of meaning that implies complexity and order… the opposite of chaos… and *cosmology* is the study of the natural order of the universe. To have *universal mastery* is to know that you have the entire life force of the universe inside of you and being a free and open channel of that force flowing through you.

The fundamentals of the cosmos are the same as the hallmarks of universal mastery – harmony, balance, order and unity – and those who embody these make wise and compassionate decisions that positively impact self, others and the cosmos. In other words, their very existence is a beacon of light with no further action necessary.

Naturally, this does not mean that they don't take any action, it simply means they can choose not to because they know on the deepest level that they don't need to in order for life to have meaning. They know that they are life and that is enough.

"Instead of asking, what do I want from life,
a more powerful question is,
what does life want from me?"

-

Eckhart Tolle

As the Hopi tribe of North America have prophesied, 'we are the ones we are waiting for'. We are the purpose, the cause and the effect. Our presence is all that is necessary and then it's up to us what to co-create. That depends on what we want to realise as well as how we want to express ourselves as individuals and as an integral part of the whole; the contribution we want to make. But broadly speaking and in the words of one of the elders… it is the pure joy of the presence of You… of being, 'I am ____' , with the freedom to choose in each moment how to fill in the blank. It is the *reALLisation* of all aspects of self and of life. The understanding that we are both the player and the playing field.

Whatever it is that you think eludes you is already yours, including abundance. The source of all abundance is not outside of you, it's a part of you and it's *gratitude*; the acknowledgement of the good that is already in your life and of the abundance that is all around you, that awakens the dormant abundance within.

"For to the one who has, more will be given, and
from the one who has not, even what he has will
be taken away."

-

Jesus of Nazareth

You don't need to own a lot, in fact you don't need to own anything to feel abundant. Although it's absolutely true that if you do *feel* consistently abundant on the inside, abundance will almost certainly flow to you on the outside too. It seems unkind, almost cruel, that abundance seems to flow easily to those who already have it and elude those who do not. But it isn't cruel, it's universal law in action. Abundance and scarcity are simply inner states that eventually manifest in outer reality. The universe has no opinion about which you choose and will deliver either to you. As you wish.

Whatever you believe other people are withholding from you – acknowledgement, appreciation, love, respect – give it to them unconditionally. In other words, behave as if you have already received it from them and expect nothing more in return. At the same time, start to see and acknowledge the generosity of nature and abundance of the world around you... the warmth of the sun, the beauty of flowers, the succulence of fruit, the power of a waterfall, the richness of your coffee, the density of the forest. When our actions are driven by universal love and a feeling of abundance, we have personal *sovereignty* and *agency* as the author of our life. But it's a very rare human being indeed who can claim to be living in this state of universal mastery all the time. It comes and it goes, fading in and out of our awareness like a desert mirage but just one glimpse of it, is enough for us to know it's there. A part of our reality that is always available to us. It's not the reserve of the chosen few who are born for greatness. Nothing could be further from the truth.

REALISATION PRACTICE: *Universal Love In Action*

This practice involves working with one other person or in a small group of family or friends. The aim is to help build the capacity to act from *Source*, by sensing what wants to happen in the present moment through universal love. It invites us to share with others our inner experience, whatever it is, right now in the present moment. You can choose any topic without limit, the only rules are honesty and transparency. We're not usually accustomed to this level of extreme honesty and it can feel a bit awkward at first but with practice, it gets easier. It requires you to be vulnerable and to allow it in others. When we are able to do this not only do we learn from the past. We can also learn from the future by focusing on future possibilities without fear or limitation.

To begin you must agree on a topic that is thought provoking or that causes excitement, difficulty or controversy. Depending on who is with you, it could be about moving home or changing careers, or something more abstract and nebulous like changing the world. There's no agenda and no purpose or end game other than allowing whatever happens to happen. Each person in turn shares whatever comes up for them at that moment. You simply trust, and allow what wants to happen to emerge through *dialogue.*

> "From time to time, the tribe gathered in a circle. They just talked and talked and talked apparently to no purpose. They made no decisions. There was no leader. And everybody could participate."
>
> \-
>
> *David Bohm*

In his book, On Dialogue, David Bohm continues, "*There may have been wise men or wise women who were listened to a bit more – the older ones – but everybody could talk. The meeting went on, until it finally seemed to stop for no reason at all and the group dispersed. Yet after that, everybody seemed to know what to do because they understood each other so well. Then they could get together in smaller groups and do something or decide things"*. The point that David is making is that it's not about what you say; the key to being in dialogue is to stay present, enable universal love to be expressed through you and truly *accept* everyone and everything that arises. This doesn't mean you have to *agree* with others but simply that you *understand* and accept them and in this way, together discover what wants to happen.

Here are a few questions to help you get going but don't allow these to limit whatever questions arise for you…

- What are your thoughts and feelings at this moment?
- What can you imagine at this moment?
- What's the greatest potential?
- What's possible now?
- What would love do?

MIRROR MOMENT: *The Never-Ending Journey*

Some say from the position of universal mastery there are no further questions. And the question is, do you agree with that? If not, then what questions do you have for yourself now?

SELF-ASSESSMENT

- When it comes to my spiritual well-being (SQ), where am I doing well?
- Where is there room for improvement?
- What do I want to work on?
- Where do I want to focus primarily?
- On a scale of 1-10 (10 is high) how satisfied am I with the level of my current, overall spiritual well-being?

SELF-COACHING: *What would love do?*

You will probably have identified one or more areas where you can improve your spiritual well-being. Choose which of these you want to start with and write a short opening statement that best describes it as the topic you want to focus on, as if you were going to share it with a coach. E.g. *I was born with a condition that means it's likely I will die young. I struggle with it and I want to make peace with death.* You can then repeat this process for each of the areas you want to work on.

STEP 1: What would love ask?

Imagine it's a loved one and not yourself that you're talking to and that it's *their* topic. If the aim of this step is to know what the 'other person' wants, what question/s do you want to ask in order to understand? And how would you answer each of those question/s?

STEP 2: What would love say?

Imagine it's a loved one and not yourself that you're talking to and it's *their* answer/s, what would you say in response and how would you say it?

STEP 3: What would love do?

Imagine it's a loved one and not yourself that you're talking to and it's *their* topic you are offering advice on, what would you advise them to do?

STEP 4: What stops you?

Based on this inner dialogue, what stops you from taking your own advice and acting from a place of self-love? If nothing is stopping you, then all you need to do is take action. If something is stopping you, go back to STEP 1 and repeat the cycle – but focus on your answer to this question – until you know what to do, how and when to do it, and there's nothing else stopping you.

Chapter 4

DO WELL

"The foundation of all success is to take action."

–

Pablo Picasso

We have now shared with you the magic of self-love, self-coaching and applying these principles to the well-being of your body, mind, heart and spirit. We've explained to the best of our ability, how to choose your *thoughts* and harness your *feelings* to drive the actions that will get you to where you want to be. We trust that if you've come this far, you're already experiencing many of the benefits in the here and now. This is because whatever we focus on with energy is what we tend to bring into our life. We've explored how to live a better life by listening to and acting on our higher self and manifesting what we really want. You may think we all want different things and you're right in terms of individuality, opinion, style and taste. But when it comes down to the fundamentals of life, most of us want the same things; to be happy and healthy, to have loving relationships with ourselves, each other and the planet, to have world peace and to see the end of suffering.

We have endeavoured to show how, if we want to live a better life, we can do this by working with ourselves in a holistic, integral way. For example, if we develop our intellect only, we potentially become more aware of our weaknesses and shortcomings and we become consciously incompetent in most areas of our lives, especially in matters of the heart. It's from there that we become self-critical and develop a lack of self-love. If we develop our feelings only, we can potentially become so overwhelmed by emotions, that we can't acknowledge or understand things and we lose perspective and clarity. In our experience, it's a whole lot easier to develop our hearts and minds together – physically and spiritually. The four realms of being human are intrinsically interrelated and to get well and be well in life, we need to develop all four. The ultimate purpose is to raise our personal power, to enable us to be the best version of our authentic self so that from there, we can relate to the best version of others and together, co-create a better reality. Because we tend to agree with Abraham Lincoln when he said, "*The best way to predict the future is to create it.*"

In this final chapter, we explore what it means to do well, by experiencing and appreciating our inner *wisdom* and *freedom*, which we all have access to; to help us manifest our destiny, not only as individuals, but as humanity.

WISDOM

"Knowledge is knowing that a tomato is a fruit;
wisdom is not putting it in a fruit salad."

-

Miles Kington

Wisdom is more than knowing what to do in life, it's also acting on what we know. It is how we apply knowledge in an insightful way, not only in our everyday life, but for the greatest good of all. As George Bernard Shaw once said, '*We are made wise not by the recollection of our past, but by the responsibility for our future.*' The self-help author Wayne Dyer has said that wisdom is more than just a gut feeling, it's God talking to us and therefore, a form of a guidance to be listened to and acted upon. Wisdom is our infinite treasure and nothing demonstrates this more eloquently than the following transcript of a well-known fable:

Today I want to tell you a story of a beggar. This beggar sat on the road for more than thirty years begging for pennies.

One day a man passed by the beggar... "Spare some change?" asked the beggar.
The man replied: "I have nothing to give you, but what is this thing you are sitting on?"
The beggar said: "It's an old box I've been sitting on for a long time."
"Have you tried opening it to see what is inside?" the man asked.
The beggar replied, "Of course not, there is nothing inside, it is empty."
The man insisted the beggar look inside... and to his surprise he discovered an abundance of gold and treasure.

We tend to spend most of our lives searching for wisdom when in fact, it's always *here*… deep down inside of *us*… like the ocean beneath the waves. A vast sea of infinite wisdom and unconditional love. This has always been the case but the majority of us are only now becoming aware of it. Maybe because we are, as some say, evolving to a 'higher frequency' and experiencing a *great awakening* or to put it more simply, maybe we are just growing up. We're becoming more conscious, both individually and collectively of this inner guidance and we're starting to *real-ise* – see with *real-eyes* – the abundance of gold and treasure that we are sat upon. The scales on our eyes are starting to fall away and we are seeing reality more clearly.

Nobody can tell you who you are, you can only discover this for yourself and until then you are like the beggar in the parable sitting on a box of treasure. In ancient Greece, people would flock to the Oracle at the Temple of Apollo in Delphi, to ask questions and receive guidance about their everyday lives. Others went there in search of wisdom because they understood the real meaning of the words that are inscribed above the entrance to the temple. ΓΝΩΘΙ ΣΑΥΤΟΝ, literally translated says 'know thyself' but what it really means is… *before any other question first, ask who you are.*

Knowing who you *really are goes* way deeper than being self-aware and knowing your higher self. It takes universal awareness to know who you really are. With universal awareness comes universal love, including self-love and with it, surrender, acceptance, commitment and trust. All the things, in fact, that we feel for someone else who we might describe as *the love of my life.* With self-love comes the understanding that *you* are the love of your life, the one you have been waiting for to complete *you* and being the best you in the present moment is your purpose.

The present moment has always appeared to be a very small place with very limited opportunities but this is an illusion. In fact, the ever present now is magnificent and infinite. In his seminal work, *The Power Of Now,* Eckhart Tolle explains that the present moment is ALL we have… so don't ignore it! He says, if we surrender to the present moment fully, we will discover eternal joy and peace, a place where problems never exist. The present moment doesn't just have the characteristics of eternity, it is eternity… a magical place where everything and anything both reside and are possible and it feels like home. It's the homecoming to the unconditional, it's as familiar and welcoming as the smell of home baked bread. Sometimes called *Source,* the field of pure potential is both *what it is* and *what it is for.* It is where being and doing both merge to become one in what is quite literally an alchemical reaction. *Being* and *doing* don't just happen simultaneously, they become the same thing. This is because at Source, time and space don't exist. How could they when *now* and *infinity* are one and the same thing? When we tap into this wisdom, we intuitively know what to do in the moment – there is no time delay. From here we have the benefit of hindsight in the present moment. We don't need to have much of an inner dialogue, all we need to do is ask *what would love do?* Our thoughts, feelings and behaviour intuitively align and we automatically experience and express wisdom and love in action. We embrace our true selves and realise in the moment that we are already complete and perfect. We act authentically, which means we don't avoid, deny, pretend or escape. Instead we face life, find strength in our vulnerability and we have the courage to do well. When we are guided by wisdom and love and not fear, we are courageous enough to take full responsibility for our lives, not for what happens to us, but how we respond. We believe that authenticity is the expression of the greatest love of all… self-love… and is the key to the end of human suffering. That's why we want you to know who you really are. That's why we want you to feel *Loved.*

We know from quantum physics that everything we perceive as form is in fact, a mass of atomic particles vibrating at such a high frequency that they appear to be solid. That includes us. We also know that if it were not for gravity, magnetic fields and all other atmospheric elements that conspire to create polarity, there would be no spaces in between the particles and therefore, no separation. Form in all of its forms cannot exist as separate entities and the existence and experience of ALL that is, in the form of life as we know it, could not have happened.

In this universal paradigm of interconnectivity in the present moment and the field of potential, there is a *reALLisation* of all that is, was and ever will be. We are both the experience and the expression of this.

"At the deepest level of Being,
you are one with all that is."

-

Eckhart Tolle

Now, all of this may sound 'out there' to you but that's an illusion too. The phrase *as above so below* was inscribed upon the Emerald Tablet by Hermes Trismegistus and embraces the entire system of traditional and modern magic. The *macrocosmos* is the same as *microcosmos*, and as Carl Sagan put it in Cosmos, '*The nitrogen in our DNA, the calcium in our teeth, the iron in our blood, the carbon in our apple pies were made in the interiors of collapsing stars. We are made of starstuff.*' The universe and everything in it, is one and the same thing. And it turns out that we have a crucial part to play in life; a part that requires no acting but simply being ourselves. *Authenticity* is our only job in whatever we do. Through being ourselves and loving ourselves unconditionally, we create a healthy relationship with ourselves primarily, then with the world. We could all benefit from better relationships, within families, our circle of friends, our enemies, political leaders and countries. People are also starting to realise that the planet is desperate for us to have a healthy relationship with it. It is our responsibility to *get well, be well* and *do well,* to co-create a better life for ALL! This paradigm provides opportunities for transformation on every level, increased connectivity and co-creation on a global scale. We are now being invited to see 'reality' for what it really is and the fact that we're both the expression and the experience of Source. It's not that we can co-create our reality and destiny, we are already co-creating reality and our destiny. The aim of this book is to help you to open up to this and act on it with wisdom and love.

Wisdom is an awareness that all *things* come and go in this present moment, there is a sense of peace, optimism, resilience, harmony and balance. Life's *problems* can be experienced as life's *lessons* and we can be grateful for all of life's ups and downs. Wisdom can be acquired through experience and by being open to the inherent insight contained within it and therefore, within ourselves. Becoming the best version of you is synonymous with being your authentic Self. This can take time and no time at all, depending on how we experience it. One day, we feel on top of the world, in flow, in tune with our higher self and fully *loved.* The next day, we feel, well, a bit shit! The truth is, most of us experience glimpses of wisdom and it's in these moments of lucidity, that we remember what it feels like to be our true Self, happy and at peace with who we are – perfectly imperfect. But what about the times when we forget that being ourselves is good enough? This is our journey of Self-discovery and we will always need to keep on working on our self and with our Self, in order to tap into our innate wisdom and feel fully *loved.* It is the never ending journey of co-creation; reflecting on our experiences, our inner dialogue, the relationship we have with ourselves, and becoming more conscious of what our body, mind, heart and spirit are telling us and becoming more open to new ways of thinking, feeling and behaving. Wisdom bestows on us an unwavering respect for ourselves, each other and the planet. No wise act is ever selfish. True altruism is not giving to others out of the goodness of our heart. It's when we understand that what we do for others, we do for ourselves – the common good is our good – how can it be otherwise when we are all one? The wisdom of *reALLisation* – that we are *ALL one* and not *alone* in life – enables us to *get well* and *be well.* From this space, we can end our suffering and *do well* for all.

Many great spiritual teachers through the ages have shown us many different paths to enlightenment, all leading to the same place. Of these, there was one who shared his insights in the form of his Dhamma to show us The Way and another who said *"I Am The Way... follow me"*. For us, these two quite distinct paths are just different routes to the same destination – whether you call it bliss, paradise, ecstasy, nirvana or heaven and there are many others. Whatever our own background, personal preference or bias, the integral lens – through which everything contains a partial truth – enables us to learn as much as possible from all our spiritual teachers including Buddha, who showed us the way forward through knowledge and clarity of mind and Jesus, who showed us the way forward through love of the unconditional kind and purity of heart.

What's fascinating is that both paths, as described here, are one and the same and both lead to *freedom.* They are only different when seen from the perspective of ego, which can only perceive things through the lens of polarity. Universal Awareness enables us to see that they are both a part of the same whole. From here, we see the ebb and flow of life and we understand that our fear of death is in fact fear of separation and that, is an illusion. There is no death and there is no separation. It is one of life's saddest ironies that when we most need to hold this truth close to our hearts, is when we find it most difficult. When a loved one departs this life, it can be devastating. We fear that what we can't see or hear no longer exists. Everything is black including our clothes. Why do we do that? This too is a part of the experience and the mystery of life.

"Wisdom is knowing I am nothing,
Love is knowing I am everything,
and between the two my life moves."
-
Nisargadatta Maharaj

With universal awareness comes the wisdom that love is a universal truth and that is unalterable, eternal and unambiguous. It can be unrecognised, but it cannot be changed. Love applies to everyone and everything. It has no opposite, no beginning and no end. It merely is. The source of love is abundant in the everlasting now. It's not outside us, it is part of who we are and wisdom knows this. If we can align our thoughts, feelings and behaviours with infinite, unconditional love, we can together create a reality that feels *loved* for everyone.

"Humans are actually spirit beings
who each possess a mind and a body and
what we do with them is entirely up to us."
-
Vaughan Jones

Wisdom and love give rise to *discernment,* the ability to make good judgments and decisions. We can choose, from moment-to-moment, how to respond to life and more importantly, how to co-create it. If we could choose a *better life* for us, what would we choose? We have the freedom to start again if we choose to; our financial systems, how we do business, how we deal with poverty, health, education, equality etc.. We can start by starting again within our relationships with each other and with ourselves. All of this is beautifully expressed in one of our favourite quotes from the extraordinary time when the world shut down in 2020…

"We will not go back to normal.
Normal never was. Our pre-corona existence
was never normal other than we normalized
greed, inequity, exhaustion, depletion,
extraction, disconnection, confusion, rage,
hoarding, hate and lack.
We should not long to return, my friends.
We are being given the opportunity to stitch a new
garment. One that fits all of humanity and nature."

-

Sonya Renee Taylor

Having discernment enables us to choose what serves us and our planet. The ability to choose brings with it liberation from victimhood and the *freedom* that we've been waiting for all our lives.

FREEDOM

"The one thing you can't take away from me is the way I choose to respond to what you do to me."

-

Viktor E. Frankl

Freedom is the ultimate achievement of man, because no matter what life throws at us, even through immense suffering, we always have the inner freedom to choose our response and to remain true to ourselves. Therefore, the meaning of life is not found on some mountain top, rather it is revealed from moment-to-moment in our choices. It's true that many of the wisest people have become so through surviving traumatic events and have lived to tell the tale of their 'spiritual awakening'. For the rest of us, our development is incremental. Ultimately, working to improve our well-being in all four realms and as a result, tapping into unconditional love and our innate wisdom, always leads us eventually to freedom. Freedom from suffering caused by the belief that we are separate from Source and from having our ego in the driving seat. Freedom from the mundane, from the past, from illusion; freedom from fear, anxiety, depression, denial and a whole host of other defence mechanisms that keep us enslaved in suffering. The freedom to choose how we engage with reality, based on the present moment rather than past conditioning, unconscious beliefs and associations. An absolute freedom that only comes from realising that we and everything in this universe are one.

As with wisdom, freedom is right here within us. There's no technique or belief that's needed to *get there* because it's *always here* and once we tap into wisdom and love, we naturally start to acknowledge the freedom we already have. We respect the past and yet, we are not tied to it. We're free to stop what we're doing, especially if it's not working for us and to literally *start again.* And when we do 'the work' to *get well* and *be well,* we will be in a better position to *do well...* together. We could then, with our hand on our heart, say that *we do what we love and love what we do.*

"Love what you do and do what you love. Don't listen to anyone else who tells you not to do it. You do what you want, what you love."

-

Ray Bradbury

Ray Bradbury wasn't the only one to advise this, Confucius famously said *"Choose a job you love, and you will never have to work a day in your life,"* and Steve Jobs said *"The only way to do great work is to love what you do"*. Of course, these insights don't only apply to work if you don't love what you are doing in life. Whatever it is, then it's time to reorient yourself by asking... *what would love do?* You may be thinking this could be painful or disruptive. For example, you might end up considering leaving your family to travel the world. If this is the case, ask yourself, why do I stay with my family, is it out of love or out of fear? If your answer is love, you can continue to be with your family in the knowledge that it's your conscious choice to do so and it feels good. Not a sacrifice that feels bad. And you can always see the world later on in life! If you realise that you're staying out of fear, the next question is to identify the fear and if, after a lot more self-coaching and heart-to-hearts with yourself and your family you do choose to go travelling, it will be a conscious choice made from wisdom, love and freedom. If the answer is that you love travelling more, then maybe you should go because as harsh as it sounds, you do have the freedom to choose this if you really love it more. If the answer is that you love them both equally and you are torn between the two, then consider how you might achieve both. How can you love your decision to choose one over another?

There's a lot to dislike about the world we were born into. It's a world in which, as the Buddha noted, our natural way of seeing and of being, leads us to suffer and to inflict suffering on others. Still, it's also a world in which wisdom, love, authenticity, truth and happiness can align and a world that (when you start to realise that alignment), appears more beautiful, more ordered and less chaotic. And this is something to marvel at.

We are human beings not human doings and yet, paradoxically, we do really well when we become aware of this. We may well feel disheartened by the current state of the world. We may wonder what to do, we may feel small in comparison to the big problems we all face and we may think how on earth are we going to clear up all this mess? Then we may need to start small, focus on what we can do rather than what we can't; think globally while acting locally and in our everyday experiences, be what we want to see in the world. If all this sounds like a load of clichés to you, then all we can say is… you're right! But that doesn't render them worthless – deep down we all know it's true. And when you forget and act from your ego, then forgive yourself, learn from the experience, reconnect with your higher *Self* and start again.

Being ourselves is so simple, yet so difficult and so important. The hidden truth is that *we are the ones we have been waiting for* and we just don't realise it. If any of this sounds illogical, then just imagine it's not because as Einstein told us… *logic will get you from A to B, but imagination will get you everywhere else.* The power of imagination can change your life and it can change the world and often does, one person, one organism, at a time…

"The metamorphosis from a caterpillar to a butterfly can be a compelling metaphor for personal and collective transformation. The caterpillar doesn't 'work at' becoming a butterfly; it transforms in harmony with its pre-existing nature."

-

Jamie Smart

The story of the caterpillar and the butterfly is just one of many wonderful stories of transformation from the world of nature that we can draw from as we reflect on our personal journey. It's also a wonderful illustration of how we transform and transcend as a whole. Many have told this story but none have done so quite so beautifully as the developmental biologist, Dr Bruce Lipton, in his book *The Biology of Belief.* He reveals to us the dance of biology, psychology and spirituality and makes a compelling argument that beliefs exercise greater control over human biology than DNA and inheritance.

"Imagine for a moment that you are a single cell among millions of cells that together comprise a growing caterpillar... the structure around you has been operating like a well-oiled machine, and the larva world has been creeping along predictably. Then one day, the machine begins to shudder and shake. The system begins to fail. Cells begin to commit suicide. There is a sense of darkness and impending doom.

From within the dying population of cells, a new breed of cells begins to emerge called imaginal cells. Clustering in the community they collaborate to devise a plan to create something entirely new from the wreckage. Out of the decay arises a great flying machine, a butterfly, which enables the survivor cells to escape from the ashes and experience a beautiful new world.

And here is the amazing and wonderful thing: the caterpillar and the butterfly have the exact same DNA. They are literally the same organism but are receiving and responding to a different organising signal. That is where we are today. When we read the newspaper and watch the evening news, we see media reporting a caterpillar world. And yet everywhere, human imaginal cells are awakening to a new possibility. They are clustering, communicating, collaborating, and tuning in to a new coherent signal of Love."

This ability to imagine and manifest a new reality fuelled by wisdom and love gives rise to our liberation as human beings. A *freedom* to start again, together and co-create a world that we really want… a world that's *Loved.*

Love is all there is.